Royal Marines in the First World War

Royal Marines in the First World War

By Sea, By Land, By Air

Matthew Richardson

Pen & Sword
MILITARY

First published in Great Britain in 2024 by
Pen & Sword Military
An imprint of Pen & Sword Books Limited
Yorkshire – Philadelphia

Copyright © Matthew Richardson 2024

ISBN 978 1 39907 964 8

The right of Matthew Richardson to be identified as
Author of this Work has been asserted by him in accordance
with the Copyright, Designs and Patents Act 1988.

A CIP catalogue record for this book is
available from the British Library

All rights reserved. No part of this book may be reproduced or
transmitted in any form or by any means, electronic or mechanical
including photocopying, recording or by any information storage and
retrieval system, without permission from the Publisher in writing.

Typeset by Mac Style
Printed in the UK by CPI Group (UK) Ltd, Croydon, CR0 4YY.

Pen & Sword Books Limited incorporates the imprints of After
the Battle, Atlas, Archaeology, Aviation, Discovery, Family History,
Fiction, History, Maritime, Military, Military Classics, Politics,
Select, Transport, True Crime, Air World, Frontline Publishing, Leo
Cooper, Remember When, Seaforth Publishing, The Praetorian Press,
Wharncliffe Local History, Wharncliffe Transport, Wharncliffe True
Crime and White Owl.

For a complete list of Pen & Sword titles please contact:

PEN & SWORD BOOKS LIMITED
47 Church Street, Barnsley, South Yorkshire, S70 2AS, England
E-mail: enquiries@pen-and-sword.co.uk
Website: www.pen-and-sword.co.uk
or
PEN AND SWORD BOOKS
1950 Lawrence Road, Havertown, PA 19083, USA
E-mail: uspen-and-sword@casematepublishers.com
Website: www.penandswordbooks.com

Contents

Acknowledgments   vi
Introduction   vii

Chapter 1   Ostend and Antwerp 1914   1
Chapter 2   Gallipoli and the Dardanelles 1915   26
Chapter 3   Sea Service 1914–1918   53
Chapter 4   The Western Front 1916–1918   86
Chapter 5   The Zeebrugge Raid 1918   112
Chapter 6   Russia 1918–1919   124
Chapter 7   Flying Marines   133

Notes   145
Bibliography   149
Index   151

Acknowledgments

In compiling this book I have drawn upon images from a range of sources. I must in particular pay tribute to my late friend Patrick Gariepy who shared a number of his photographs before his untimely passing. I must also thank another longstanding friend, John Caley, for his assistance in improving the quality of a number of the images which appear herein.

J.A. Brough, author of *A Marine in the Great War*, could not be traced, but acknowledgment is made to him as the source of the image of John Brough, which appears herein. Likewise the owner of the photograph of Tom Pyle could not be traced, though acknowledgement of copyright is hereby made, and thanks expressed to both parties.

As always, any errors of fact or interpretation are my own.

Matthew Richardson, Douglas, 2024

Introduction

On 28 October 1914 the Corps of Royal Marines celebrated the 250th anniversary of its formation. Centuries ago, regiments of soldiers were carried aboard the king's ships, for the purposes of combat. 'Shipmen', as sailors were then called, were hired only for the duration of the voyage, and it was believed at the time that they should do the navigating, whilst soldiers did the fighting. Eventually the full-time Royal Navy evolved, and out of the practice of taking soldiers on board grew the Corps of Marines, which latterly was granted its Royal title. Early-twentieth-century Royal Marines were organised into two branches: that of the Royal Marine Light Infantry (RMLI), and that of the Royal Marine Artillery. The infantrymen wore the traditional red coats and were referred to as 'red marines', while the artillerymen with their blue coats were called 'blue marines'. The Royal Marine Light Infantry was organised into three divisions, each located near one of the principal naval bases at Chatham, Portsmouth, and Plymouth, with a depot at Walmer (Deal). These divisions provided a manpower pool for shipboard marine detachments and for expeditionary forces in time of war or emergency. The Royal Marine Artillery had a single division located at Eastney near Portsmouth.

Although the Royal Marine Artillery was a gunnery corps, its men were also trained to do infantry work. They practiced musketry, and were also drilled to handle every kind of artillery, from the light quick-firer to the big barbette gun. In addition to that, they were taught repository work, which meant shifting, mounting and dismounting guns by means of improvised derricks. Every battleship and large cruiser carried a detachment of Royal Marine Artillery as part of its crew, and although their work did not differ substantially from that of the seaman gunners, they had their own messes and officers.

The Royal Marine Light Infantry were intended to form landing parties, and small expeditionary forces when required to deal with trouble on shore. All larger ships carried a detachment, and certain special duties fell to them. It was a Marine sentry who struck the hours on a ship's bell. A Marine sentry was always on duty beside the lifebuoy, which he was to launch immediately if he heard the cry, 'Man Overboard'. Marines kept order, and if a sailor gave trouble a party of them would escort him below. Lastly they were much in evidence for ceremonial duties, and Royal Marine bandsmen would both provide accompaniment for tasks such as coaling, and also a musical salute for visiting dignitaries. As a 'soldier and a sailor too', the Marine was equally useful in either capacity, and had an adaptability that neither the soldier nor the sailor possessed. The journalist E. Charles Vivian, writing in 1915, expanded further on this:

> From this brief summary of the work of the Royal Marines two or three inevitable conclusions arise. First of these is the unending interest of the work. An infantryman trains to a certain routine, and there he ends. He can go on perfecting himself in his work, developing himself, but there is no unending list of new things such as is at the command of the Marine, who is infantryman, artilleryman, and generally sailor as well by training. The driving forces of the soldier are discipline and initiative, or perhaps it might be better put as discipline backed by initiative; the driving force of the sailor is handiness – he has to get things done and he gets them done; but the Marine, hybrid by training, has to combine discipline, initiative, and handiness with uncanny quickness in getting things done, and it is safe to say that there is more scope for intelligence in the Royal Marines than in any branch of either Navy or Army. Given average intelligence and the desire to learn, the man in the Marines has more chance of fitting himself for and taking promotion than any other man. As an instance of this, at the outbreak of war the Royal Marines furnished a number of instructors to the Army, and many of those men have already been granted commissions from the unit to which they were sent.
>
> Yet another point with regard to this diversity of training is the fitness of men for almost any kind of employment on their return to civil life. Infantry, cavalry, or artillery, on putting off uniform are still soldiers by habit; the Marine, having been everything and

done everything, is able to take up any form of civilian work as easily as he turned from the use of a big gun to the repair of a field telephone or the running of a motorcar. And the popularity of the Marine service among the men who have served is evidenced by the fact that generation after generation of a family enrolls, while not infrequently father and sons are serving at the same time in the same corps. The second conclusion is the value of the work. Ultimately, the very bread we eat is dependent on the shooting ability of the Marine and his kind, for there is not a capital ship in the Navy that is without Marines to man its guns, and on those guns depend the national food supply – and the life of the nation itself. Coast defence service, anti-aircraft service, service with the big guns, and as an Infantry Brigade in France and in the Dardanelles, are all part of the vital work of guarding the Empire, auxiliary to that maintenance of sea power with which the Royal Marines have always been so closely connected.

From a patriotic standpoint, there is no higher form of service than with the Royal Marines. And then, a last conclusion, there is the spirit in which the men are trained, and the resulting spirit of the men themselves. One may see these things in the classes training at gun-laying, where every man knows that the score on his card must be good, for the credit of the corps of which he is a member; in the squads swinging out to drill, made up of finely developed, bronzed, healthy-looking men, from which the best is asked and by whom the best is given, for the credit of the corps: in the care, the individual instruction, the study of the best methods, with which every instructor devotes himself to his task, for the credit of the corps; in the disciplined efficiency evident at every turn, by reason of which the Royal Marines consider themselves – and with justice – the finest body of men in the British Forces. It is a corps of great traditions: of unequalled distinctions. It is 'nobody's child', soldiers trained for sea service, and sailors ashore, capable of doing the work of both. This lack of official parentage has given rise to self-reliance and self-sufficiency, so that whatever arises to be done, the Marine can do it. In their work and their manner of doing it, as in the matter of pre-eminence in sport, the Marines yield place to none; the man who joins this corps is not only fitting himself for service with the best trained body of men that the Navy and Army possess, but he is also educating himself in the ways that will be useful for the rest of his life.[1]

Evidence of the high state of morale of the Royal Marines, and their identification with their cause, comes from a letter from Sergeant B.J. Fielder who wrote to his wife on 17 August 1914:

> If I go away you must not worry if you don't get my letters, because you must understand it is all for the Good of England, and the English soldier is not only fighting for his country but to save his own home from destruction and being ruled over by the Germans.[2]

Lest this viewpoint should be considered singular, his conviction was shared by another Marine, Private George Bird, writing home around the same time:

> Poor Florrie, I was sorry to read of her crying about me. It is a matter of duty this war. I am out to save our home and you, the same as millions more are doing.[3]

Even after the true scale of the casualties in this war was becoming painfully apparent, there was still a quiet resilience and a determination to see it through. Private Bert Williamson, one of the Royal Marines aboard HMS *Highflyer*, in a letter to his parents at 4, Hare Lane, Gloucester, told them not worry about him:

> If we should go under you will know it was for a good cause. I am not afraid to die ... I see my regiment lost a lot men at the Dardanelles.[4]

So important to the war effort were the Royal Marines considered to be, that as early as November 1914 an amendment was made to the Royal Marines Act of 1847, so that whereas previously if a man's term of service had expired whilst on a foreign station, it might be prolonged, that provision was now extended to any port or station. Regular soldiers could not be similarly compelled to continue to serve beyond the expiry of their allotted time until the passing of the Military Service Act of 1916.

The book that you are about to read explores the extraordinary versatility displayed by the men of the Royal Marines at war between 1914 and 1918. In war on land – from the jungles of Africa, to the beaches of Gallipoli; from the trenches of France to the steppes of Russia. In war at sea – from mighty battleships to lowly merchant men, from gun turrets to storming parties. Finally in the air, as pioneers of the newest form of combat. Never was a cap badge more appropriately worn than the globe and laurel of the Royal Marines.

Chapter One

Ostend and Antwerp 1914

Shortly after the outbreak of the First World War, in the early morning of 27 August 1914 a landing by two battalions of Royal Marines took place at the Belgian port of Ostend; two further battalions joined them the next day (the Chatham, Portsmouth and Plymouth RMLI battalions together with a Royal Marine Artillery battalion now making up the Royal Marine Brigade.) These men were mostly reservists recalled to the colours. Colour Sergeant Thomas Bilson remembered the irrepressible humour of the British Tommy which was to show itself time and again in this war:

Marines landing stores at Ostend, 1914. (*Author's Collection*)

> We were disembarking at Ostend in 1914. Each man was expected to carry as much stores as he could. One Cockney Marine was struggling down the gangway – full marching order, rifle slung round his neck, kitbag under his arm, and a box in each hand. As he balanced the boxes we heard him mutter, 'S'pose, if I juggle this lot orlright they'll poke annuver in my mouf.'[1]

The primary purpose of the operation was to safeguard a British seaplane base located there, but the Marines were ordered to hold the town until Belgian troops who had retreated into France could be transferred, and 4,000 Belgian troops duly arrived on 30 August. The rapid Allied retreat led the War Office to decide that supplies would have to be brought through ports in western France, as the existing arrangements in the Pas-de-Calais ports were too exposed. This would be more demanding on naval escort ships, leaving too few to support the force at Ostend. Thus after this short foray ashore, the Marines were re-embarked and returned to their ports. Major General Sir George Aston had organised the operation and commanded the force, and recalled that it also had a counter intelligence purpose:

> The outstanding occurrences which were most helpful were the 'Russian troops rumour' (about mysterious Russians arriving in Scottish ports and travelling southward by night) and the news that the Belgian division, driven out of Namur, was embarking at Havre and coming round to Ostend. The Russian-troops rumour, told me by the correspondent of the Times, was very useful. My marines were dressed in blue, with round caps with no peaks. They might easily be taken for Russians by German spies. Crowds of civilians were traveling through Ostend for the south and spying was very easy. I hoisted my huge union jack in the railway-station for them to report, and I took care that the Russian-troops rumour was told as a strict secret to as many people as possible. That is the best way to make sure of wide publicity; but although I heard afterwards that the rumour was believed by vast numbers of people in England, I thought at the time that it was almost too much to hope for its belief by experts in the German General Staff.[2]

Around the same time, 150 officers and men of the RMLI together with 50 RMA were sent to Dunkirk to man armoured cars. They were colloquially known as the 'Motor Bandits'. Their official role was to support the Royal Naval Air Service (RNAS) units, under Commander Charles Rumney Samson, Britain's most prominent naval pilot of the years immediately before the First World War, who was also responsible for pioneering armoured fighting vehicles. He had arrived in Belgium in August 1914 initially with the Eastchurch Squadron of the Royal Naval Air Service. The squadron was sent to Belgium to provide the RNAS with a suitable base on the Continent from which it could attack the enemy; for the Marines who were sent out with this unit it was an easy posting, to begin with, at least. One of them, Sergeant B.J. Fielder, wrote to his wife in early October 1914:

> I am sending this from a little place called Cassell about 25 miles from Dunkirk and 75 miles from the scene of the actual fighting so that you can see that I am safe as houses. The only thing I don't like to think is that you are all needlessly worrying yourself about me. I only wish you would believe me that they will not send us to the Front we are being kept to look after Commander Samson's aeroplanes ... I am writing this sitting on a veranda of a small school where we are billeted.[3]

Samson however was critically short of serviceable aircraft for this primary role, but his aggressive spirit was aroused when he used two of his squadron transport cars (commandeered civilian vehicles armed with Maxim guns) to attack from 500 yards range a German staff car. Two of the enemy were wounded in the engagement and the staff car quickly turned about. Armoured cars – highly mobile and useful for causing mayhem behind enemy lines – were born.

Two days later Samson set out again with four of his cars for another foray, this time into Lille, evacuated temporarily by the enemy, to capture or destroy any German transport that he might find there. This roving commission suited Samson well and his next assignment was to support the Royal Naval Division at Antwerp. To increase their protection, a pair of his cars – a Mercedes and a Rolls-Royce – were quickly given

Commander Charles Rumney Samson RN, with some of his armoured car officers. Three of those on the right of the group are Royal Marines. (*Author's Collection*)

rudimentary armour in the form of a covering of quarter-inch boiler plate, in the dockyards of Antwerp. It was soon found however that the armour fitted was inadequate, and a heavier vehicle was required. Part of the squadron's transport consisted of commandeered London 'type B' buses. Two of these were adapted and became armoured lorries. The cab was covered with armour plate and the main body work was replaced with what was in reality an open topped armoured box with sloping sides, from which a crew of Royal Marines could fire their rifles. These vehicles were intended to act as armoured personnel carriers allowing infantry to support the operations of the lighter armoured cars. Alas the weight of the boiler plate made the armoured buses too slow to keep up with the armoured cars, and as a result they were mainly used during the Antwerp operations as mobile blockhouses guarding crossroads. One of these, used by Samson's brother Felix was further armed with a machine gun. In the course of these operations, German light field guns were encountered for the first time, and it became apparent that an armoured vehicle mounting an artillery piece was needed to support the lighter armoured cars. One of the B type buses was fitted with a three pounder naval gun. This proved successful at providing cover for the armoured cars, and two Mercedes Daimler lorries were also adapted to carry the same weapon. One eye witness who crossed paths with him remembered:

> A remarkable man called Commander Samson, who was – or had been – with a naval reserve unit, dashed on to our scene. The Commander was a little rotund, weather-beaten man, in naval uniform with a 'Captain Kettle' beard and whiskers, driving round in a Rolls-Royce armoured lorry, the size of a taxi. He had mounted on it a three-pounder gun on a pivot, and he had a sailor with him as his driver. He told us, 'We've just come out from Antwerp. Makin' ourselves a bit useful with this naval armoured car!' Round his hat he had a white band, on which he had painted, in black, '2,000

Royal Marines manning an armoured car during the Antwerp operations. They wear RMA cap badges. The vehicle is a converted London bus. (*Author's Collection*)

MARKS'. He said, 'That's the price the Germans have put on my head if they capture me.'[4]

As the German army swept through Belgium in the late summer and early autumn of 1914, the continued resistance of the citadel of Antwerp on the Belgian coast posed an increasing threat to its already stretched lines of communication. The Belgian army had previously sallied forth from the coast to attack them in the flank; fearing that the Antwerp garrison might well have the capacity to do so again, the German High Command despatched General Hans von Beseler to subdue the city. The mighty river Schelde formed a formidable barrier on the western side of the city, but to the south the river Nethe presented far less of an obstacle, and on this side and to the east it was defended by an obsolete fortress system dating from 1859. As the fate of Liége and Namur had already demonstrated in this war, Antwerp would have been able to offer little in the way of resistance to the superior German heavy guns should they be brought into action against it. However, Winston Churchill, as first lord of the Admiralty, was eager to keep the Belgian army in the game, and came up with a daring (or perhaps, as some said at the time, foolhardy) plan to attempt to bolster the resistance of Antwerp. This it was hoped would draw German forces away from the desperate fight then taking place on the river Aisne – indeed Churchill, for his part, saw Antwerp as representing the extreme left hand end of an Allied front which ran in an arc through Belgium and north western France, the right hand end of which rested

PO13391 Pte Herbert Appleton, Portsmouth Battalion, Royal Marine Light Infantry. He enlisted in 1904, and was a member of the Royal Fleet Reserve when recalled for service at Antwerp. He was hit by shrapnel there, and was also injured in the foot whilst serving with Commander Samson's armoured cars. (*Author's Collection*)

upon the Aisne battlefield. Churchill himself was to spend two days at Antwerp, personally superintending the defence.

About three weeks after their initial withdrawal, the Royal Marine Brigade now arrived at Dunkirk, with orders to assist the Belgians in the defence of Antwerp. By this point it was part of the hastily formed Royal Naval Division, being joined by two brigades of naval ratings. Unlike the naval battalions, which had colourful names such as Collinwood and Nelson, reflecting the heroes of the past, the Royal Marine battalions were simply numbered 9th, 10th, 11th and 12th. Many of the members of the Royal Marine Brigade were recalled reservists, some of them of many years' standing. One of these men, Private Fred Shaw had been in the Royal Marine Light Infantry some sixteen years, and had previously been stationed in China, and also in the East Indies. He saw active service in Somaliland in 1904, and was awarded a medal for that expedition. Prior to the outbreak of the First World War he had been managing his mother's business for four years, but went up to Chatham each July for his annual training. He had only returned from Chatham a week when war was declared with Germany, and he was the first man from his home town of Winsford to see active service. The Marines had their first taste of warfare at Antwerp, and it was here that Shaw was to be wounded in the back, stomach and shoulder. He made a good recovery, however, and would see combat again the following year. Private Edward Page was another of the Marine reservists who was recalled to the colours when Britain mobilised its navy just prior to the declaration of war. He wrote afterwards:

> Arriving at Dunkirk in the early hours of Sunday, 20th September 1914, we disembarked in the afternoon, and were warmly received by the inhabitants of the town, upon whom we were billeted. Our stay amongst them was not a very long one, however, and after a few days we left, part of the brigade proceeding to Lille, the remainder to Cassel, my company being included with those who went to the latter town. Our stay here was a very brief one, for on the morning of Saturday, 3rd October, we received sudden orders to entrain. By the atmosphere of suppressed excitement around us, the issuing of

extra ammunition and preserved rations, we felt our first brush with the Hun was not far off.

We had no idea of our destination at the commencement of the journey, but, having passed through the town of Dunkirk about noon, and finding we were following the coast in a northern direction, very early in the afternoon we were convinced the scene of our operations was to be somewhere in Belgium. All along the train route we were accorded an enthusiastic welcome by the people, particularly on our arrival at the town of Ghent. The people thronged the station platforms in thousands, very many of them distributing fruits, tobacco, and drinks amongst us. Poor people, little did they dream, on that sunny, early autumn afternoon, as they moved smilingly amongst us distributing their gifts, that ere another week had passed their fine town would be in the hands of their remorseless foe, and the fortunes of war would place them under the iron heel of the Hun invader for a number of weary years.[5]

Anthony Frederick Wilding, a former Wimbledon tennis champion, was one of fifty motor car owners who went to Antwerp with their vehicles as transport for the RND. They were given the rank of lieutenant in the Royal Marines. (*Library of Congress*)

It was at Lierre, about 5 miles from Antwerp, that the Marines first came into action, occupying trenches north of the Lierre-Antwerp road, and it was at that place that, to the delight of the men, First Lord of the Admiralty Winston Churchill visited them as they were about to go into the trenches; moving up and down the ranks, he addressed a few inspiring words the troops. He assured them that what was about to come would be arduous, but he was certain that they would do their duty. Dirty and unshaven, and within range of enemy fire, Churchill remained with the Marines for several days, even visiting the wounded in hospital to ask if they required cigarettes and offering his own. Edward Page continued:

> We arrived at Antwerp in the early hours of Sunday, 4th October, entering the town from the north, being immediately taken charge of by guides, who conducted us to billets, where we were enabled to snatch a few hours' sleep before leaving at daybreak to relieve Belgian troops who had been holding the line of trenches against the invader at a place called Lierre, about five miles to the south of Antwerp, and situated outside the fort defences on the main Antwerp-Brussels road. Having left the town behind us, it was not long before the distant booming of heavy pieces sounded clearer to the ear as the distance between us and Hun positions decreased, and as the day advanced the bombardment of the town increased in intensity. Shells from their large-calibre guns screeched over our heads, their flight being easily followed until they finally burst with a terrific report in the town we were leaving behind us.
>
> It has always been a matter of wonder to me how we escaped a severe shelling as we made our way down that long winding road that bright Sunday morning. Right in our path was a Hun captive balloon; the observer occupants must have detected us, but, very luckily for us, their gunners did not treat us to any special attention, and we were able to reach the trenches and relieve our Belgian comrades in arms without mishap.[6]

They stayed here from Saturday until the following Wednesday, during which period some severe fighting took place. The Marines had fifteen maxims with them, but the Germans brought their field guns into action and the British had a difficult time. On one occasion all the gunners at one German gun were put out action, and a dozen Marines were sent forward to take possession of it, but some German infantry were lying down near the gun and they shot every one of the British soldiers. Private Thomas Staite from Walsall remarked afterwards that it was like hell on earth to be in the trenches. Shells were bursting all round them, and he saw about thirty men killed or wounded with one shell, while his major got picked off with rifle fire. Unfortunately, the Marines had no artillery with them, and the Belgian guns could not reach the Germans, and so eventually the order came to retire. In consequence of the severe shell fire, the Marines had to fall back from Lierre towards Antwerp. Here again severe fighting took place.

> We arrived at last outside the outer ring of forts which defended the town, and shortly after entered the trenches held by the Belgian soldiers; and very pleased they were on our arrival, having been in the positions night and day for several days. Having taken over from them, I found our company was to hold a point of the line situated upon the main road, running between the town of Antwerp, some five miles in our rear, and the smaller town of Lierre, through which the defending line held by us ran. Directly to our front ran a small river, which had been spanned at the point we occupied by a stone bridge, this bridge having been destroyed by dynamite some days previously to prevent the Hun crossing and entering the town. All around us was the heaped-up debris from the adjoining buildings that had been brought down with the blowing up of the bridge.
>
> We were engaged during the hours of daylight in hastily improving our positions, well knowing our wily foe was not very far away, and an attack might take place at any moment. Under the supervision of our company commander, Major Shubrick, our machine-gun positions and line of trench were materially improved before night fell. It gives me the greatest pleasure to place on record the courage, devotion to duty, and great coolness displayed by this gallant officer during the short time we hung on to this part of the defending line.[7]

Major C.L. Shubrick remained at his point of observation at the head of the trench, and whilst disregarding any form of cover himself, ensured that his men took the maximum advantage of any that was available.

> During the afternoon, while we were busily engaged improving our positions, a demolition party of the Royal Engineers crossed the river and set fire to the end buildings facing us, the object being to prevent the Hun working down upon us and firing into our trenches

from their upper stories. The idea was a good one, but the smoke from the burning buildings attracted the attention of the German artillery, and just before night fell they opened fire upon us, keeping up the attack throughout the night.

With the coming day we were harassed by the attentions of their snipers, whom I have already described. Several of us volunteered to try and dislodge them from the positions they occupied. We entered the end building facing the river, and made our way up the ruined staircase to the roof. From a bedroom on the top landing we had a good view across the river of the Hun position, but they were very careful not to expose themselves, taking full advantage of the dense foliage and trees that lined the river bank. The windows and fittings had been destroyed, only part of the brick-work remaining; sand-bags had been piled up by the Belgians, but a number of these had fallen from position and lay scattered on the floor of the room.

It was impossible to replace them without giving our presence there away; it was also impossible to fire without some protection to ourselves and support for our rifles. After some time I looked round the room for something to take the place of the fallen sand-bags. Espying a large pillow lying upon the floor, I dragged it towards the opening in the brick-work where once had stood the window, and cautiously placed it in position on what remained of the sill. Resting my rifle upon it, I took aim and fired. The whole of the opening was immediately filled with flying feathers! What had happened was that, although the sights of the rifle were clear, the muzzle had sunk into the soft mass and the bullet had rent the pillow in twain. Naturally, a laugh went round the room at my expense, and I suppose I deserved it for having used the pillow as a rifle rest; but the tension on the nerves under the above circumstances is very great, and one is apt to do things without clear thought.

The smile upon the faces of my companions did not remain long, however, for the watchful eyes of the riflemen on the opposite bank had detected the sudden shower of feathers, and before they had been carried away by the breeze their place was taken by a shower of lead that poured into the room through the broken brick-work. One bullet struck a brass candlestick, shattering it to atoms, as it stood upon a small table between a comrade named Green and myself; another pill passed through the foot of a mahogany bedstead that stood in the centre of the room, splintering the woodwork, while one flying fragment cut open the face of the section corporal who was in charge. The remainder came out with a few minor scratches. We returned their fire to the best of our ability, and had the satisfaction of picking one or two of them off, their bodies rolling down the bank into the river; but our position was becoming more untenable every moment, and shortly after we were ordered to descend.

CH1366 Pte Edward Page, Chatham Battalion, who was wounded on 6 October 1914 at Lierre and taken prisoner at Antwerp. (*Author's Collection*)

About 9 a.m. the Hun succeeded in bringing into position a quick-firing gun mounted on an armoured car, and, utilising the furniture and household effects obtained from the dwellings, he was enabled to erect cover behind which it was impossible to detect his movements. Had the necessary artillery support been available, his improvised barrier would not have availed him long, but, as I have already stated and it is now well known, we were weak in artillery at this time, which gave our foe every advantage. Our rifle and machine-gun fire was, under the circumstances, almost useless, for the armoured car opening upon us at almost point-blank range, our trenches and two machine-gun positions were quickly reduced to ruins. It was now an impossibility to remain any longer, and as near as I can now remember we retired about 10 a.m., falling back to the reserve trenches about one mile in rear.[8]

Alongside the Royal Marines, men of the St John Ambulance Brigade provided additional medical support. A letter was sent to Mr Ernest

Rushworth, superintendent of the Alsager Division of the St John Ambulance Brigade, by Sergeant Major A.G. Smith, of the Royal Marine Depot, Deal, who wrote in praise of the plucky behaviour of privates Bevan and Evenson, who lived at Talke and Private Walker, of Alsager, who were recently joined members of the Royal Naval Sick Berth Reserve, from Royal Naval Ambulance Train No. 4. The letter ran as follows:

> You will perhaps be surprised to hear from me, but remembering your address, having written to you years ago in connection with our ambulance competition at Brierfield, I could not refrain from writing to tell you of the bravery of your men. The men to whom I refer are Privates Bevan, Evenson and Walker (especially Private Bevan). We were under a galling shell-fire for five days and nights at Leirre and Oude just outside Antwerp. During this time your men worked like heroes. Time after time Bevan went down to the trenches, exposed to a hail of rifle fire, together with one or two of my men, and brought back the wounded men. He was struck on the boot heel with a piece of shrapnel, but still he kept on. Many times I saw him in the thick of it – always busy, never faltering. Sir, I salute Private Bevan. Please do not let my praise of Private Bevan take any credit away from Evenson and Walker, they were amongst it also, if not quite so often as Bevan, and I never had to ask twice for men to accompany me on a hot job if they were about. What we went through is better imagined than described. The shells were falling about us, or whistling overhead at the rate of about ten a minute night and day, and our rations were bully beef and biscuits – when we could get it. No doubt your men will tell you what we went through but I thought I would drop you this note in case they should underestimate their own part in it. You have reason to be proud of your men.[9]

The journalist Sir Walter Newman Flower, in a book recounting the history and successes of the Dr Barnardo's homes, describes one incident which took place here:

For the romance of Barnardoism in the War it would be difficult to discover a better case than that of George Hall. Thirty-one years ago he came to Stepney, a youth of eighteen, on the fringe of active life, and joined the Youth's Labour House. A couple of years later he was sent to sea. This was before the days when the Barnardo boys were sent aboard the lugger, and so prepared for the sea life. There was no lugger, and so this boy had to learn the ways of the sea by the harder life afloat. To-day he is an officer holding the Distinguished Service Medal and a decoration from the Belgian Government for bravery at Antwerp.

The episode which brought him his honours happened in those terrible hours which marked the British retreat from the Belgian city. Private George Hall was in the Royal Marine Brigade, and his company was stationed in a trench on the River Nethe at Lierre, a few miles from Antwerp, and under a perfect tornado of German fire. The British reply was weak, because ammunition had been almost expended, and it seemed as if the line would have to be rapidly evacuated or every man wiped out. The officer then called for a volunteer to go for ammunition to maintain the defence. This entailed journeying across the open ground, which was swept by German fire, and back again, but the old Barnardo boy volunteered for the task.

He went out quite calmly, and made his way through the concentrated fire towards the ammunition depot. To those who watched, it seemed impossible that he would get through. But he did get through, and at the depot fetched a hand cart, loaded it up, and pushed it back across the shell-swept ground. Once he had to get the cart through a hole in the side of a house. But he brought up the ammunition untouched. If Waterloo was won on the playing fields of Eton, then of a truth it may be said that some of the greatest episodes of this War have been won on the playing fields of Barnardo's.[10]

Private George Hall was a Royal Fleet Reservist, and was 43 years old at the time of this action. Despite this glowing tribute, his character was not all that Flower might have wished for, as his service record shows three occasions in the 1890s when he was court martialled and imprisoned. None the less, his Distinguished Service Medal was gazetted on 29 December 1914, accompanied by the Croix de Guerre.

Gazetted alongside him was another DSM recipient, Quartermaster Sergeant George James Kenney, Royal Marine Light Infantry, formerly manager at the Bijou cinema, Erskine Street, Hulme, who had rejoined his regiment at the outbreak of war. Exceptionally popular with all classes of his audience, many enquiries had been made concerning him since he returned to the colours. News of his award of the Distinguished Service Medal after taking part in the operations at Antwerp was greeted with interest by cinema audiences, and enthusiastic scenes were witnessed periodically when the latest news from the front concerning the absent manager was thrown on the screen. Later it was to be announced that he had been promoted to lieutenant, and he would go on to be wounded by a shell during the desperate fighting in the Dardanelles, spending time in hospital at Malta.

The Germans however were closing the noose around Antwerp. Cavalry and other reinforcements were advancing northwards from the direction of Lens. More seriously, the forward units of the 37th Landwehr Brigade which had been closely investing the city, and which thus far had been held at bay by the Belgian army, succeeded under cover of fog in the early hours of 7 October in crossing the Schelde in boats at Schoonaerde, 9 miles above Termonde. At the same time, heavy guns were carried over the Nethe and severe bombardment of the inner line of forts commenced. That day the Royal Marine Brigade was ordered to evacuate its trenches and fall back on the Cinema Film Factory at Chateau Rouge.

The critical moment in the ill-fated defence of Antwerp came on 8 October. During the course of this day, not only did the remainder of the 37th Landwehr Brigade cross the Schelde, but it was now reinforced by the 1st Bavarian Landwehr Brigade and the 9th Ersatz Brigade. Troops of the German Marine Division were also on the Antwerp front. Heavy guns had moved closer and shells were now being directed at the city itself. The enemy increased his efforts against Forts No. 1, and No. 2, for once these had fallen to German troops, this would effectively render the continued defence of the city untenable. From this position, the Germans could fire into the rear of the other forts and cut off the retreat of their defenders. After only a few more hours of resistance, these critical forts were captured by the end of the day. Antwerp was now to be evacuated.

Private Walter Lockwood of the Plymouth Battalion, a native of Rusholme, Manchester was wounded by shrapnel in the left ankle outside Antwerp on the morning of 8 October 1914. He was taken by British Red Cross personnel to the hospital in the city, which he reached about noon the same day. At this time the hospital was staffed by Belgian doctors and nurses. Three days afterwards the hospital fell into the hands of the Germans. They replaced the Belgian doctors with their own, but kept the Belgian nurses. The Belgian surgeons had removed the piece of shrapnel when he first arrived (without anaesthetic) but now the wound was infected. About three weeks later the German doctors opened it to

The retreat from Antwerp, 1914. Belgian troops in the foreground, Royal Marines aboard the London buses in the rear. (*Library of Congress*)

clean it, and this was repeated six times under anaesthetic. The German doctors were humane and kind in their treatment, and it was to be June 1915 before he left the hospital for another at Cologne. Here the wound continued to give problems and though he could walk with the aid of a stick, once again it was opened under anaesthetic by kind and humane German doctors. The food was also good in the hospitals. Later Lockwood was transferred to Stendal prisoner of war camp, where the food was very poor. Another Marine who was taken prisoner here, on 9 October, was Private J. Chandler, who is recorded as being 58 years of age at the time. He recounted afterwards:

> I was captured at Antwerp with the Naval Brigade ... previous to my capture I saw no case of infraction by the enemy of the laws of war. I was unwounded, and was detained three days only in a church in a village, the name of which I do not know. We went straight to Döberitz Camp in Germany. The journey took three days and nights, during which we were very badly treated by our military guard. We only had two small meals during the journey, and were only allowed out of the train twice in this time. Civilians had nothing to do with us. We travelled in cattle trucks, which were very dirty and very crowded. We saw no German Red Cross officials during the journey.[11]

With him was Private Alban Charles Tully of Ryde, Isle of Wight, captured the same day. Tully had lost his great coat before he was taken prisoner, but many others who still had them saw these items taken off them by the Germans. None of Tully's party had a greatcoat when they arrived at the camp. Döberitz at first was just a large field surrounded by a barbed wire fence. Initially the prisoners lived in tents, despite the worsening winter weather. By December, wooden huts had been constructed to house the prisoners, these were heated by stoves, but there was little in the way of fuel. Another member of the Royal Fleet Reserve was Private H. Bell. He recounted in a report:

> I was serving in the Naval Division and was wounded on October 8th 1914, at Antwerp. The Germans took over the hospital on the

11th October. I went from Antwerp to a hospital at Cologne, and from there to a camp at Stendal ... It took about 36 hours to get to Cologne. We were in an ordinary train (not a Red Cross train), but were treated as well as could be expected for prisoners. On arriving at Cologne we were taken to a hospital called the Kaiserin-Agusta-Schule. In the hospital at Cologne the treatment was fair. The wounds were not dressed unless a request was made that they should be. The food was rather poor.[12]

Sixteen-year-old Bugler Heber Chappell was also captured on 9 October. He recounted:

I surrendered with the others at the fall of Antwerp. We were roughly handled after capture, but not myself particularly. We were taken to a church near Antwerp for two days and here the food we had was soup and bread, and then we were taken to Doberitz, which was reached on, I think the 15th. We walked to Termonde and entrained there. We only had the food the Belgians gave us on the journey and a slice of bread at one station and some soup at Hannover. The guards were pretty decent, and tried to get what they could for us.[13]

In order to escape, the rest of the Marine Brigade marched from 20:00 one night until 09:00 the next morning, when they reached St Gilles. From there they went by train to Ostend, and there were more men top of the train and hanging on to it than there were inside. Private Bell, of the Royal Marines, in a letter describing exciting journey from Antwerp to Ostend, wrote:

CH18840 Pte Philip Gouldsmith, from Broxbourne, Hertfordshire. He re-enlisted for the Chatham Battalion, Royal Marine Light Infantry in September 1914 (having served previously). He was interned at Groningen, Holland, following the fall of Antwerp. (*Pat Gariepy*)

We joined a train with some refugees some miles outside the city, and after we had gone several miles we found ourselves surrounded with Germans. We left the train, and Major French in command of the 10th Battalion, was asked to surrender, to which he replied, 'Surrender be damned, Royal Marines were never known to surrender.' He called us to cut our way through, and so we did, but we lost heavily, as only 190 came out of the scrap. The others were either killed, wounded, or taken prisoners.[14]

Many other men had narrow escapes. Mr Charles Franklin, the *London Express* correspondent, at Amsterdam, recounted a story told by an interned Belgian officer:

The commandant of the Belgian pontoon engineers, tells me a thrilling story of the rescue of British marines on the fall of Antwerp. The great pontoon bridges built on the Scheldt by Belgian engineers had been blown up when appeals came from the right bank of the Scheldt from some hundreds of British marines who had been cut from their brigade and wanted to cross the river to escape from the oncoming Germans. The commandant of the pontoon engineers had lost 220 of his 250 men as that number had been ordered to re-join the retiring Belgian army. German shells were falling in the river, but the commandant, with his thirty men, bravely gathered all the tugs, barques, and pleasure boats they could get together near Sainte Anne, and in less than twenty minutes he saved the British marines. The same gallant officer, with his brave engineers, afterwards went off in a tug to the Gneisenau, a North German Lloyd steamer in the harbour, and destroyed her machinery rendering her useless. He tried all night on the river in a tug with lights extinguished to find a way along to safety with his, thirty men but at last was obliged to enter Dutch territory.[15]

In Walsall, news had been received that Private J. Bird, of the Royal Marines, was also amongst those who entered Holland after the fall of Antwerp, and was interned there. In a letter to his mother, who lived at 48 Brace Street, Walsall, Private Bird said:

I am going on all right. I expect you have been thinking how I have been getting on. To tell you the truth we have had a very hard time of it, and we are very lucky to be alive. We were in Antwerp, and now I expect it is all burnt down, the Germans were firing on us there for days and nights. You can tell—we were in the trenches for three days and three nights without a wink of sleep. All the people cleared out of Antwerp, and the place is on fire. I never want to go through the same thing again. I will tell you all about when come home, but I don't know when that will be. We are prisoners in Holland, and they might keep us till the war is over … I should like you to send the football paper and some Woodbines, as we cannot got anything, and we don't get any money either. All our clothes have been burnt, and all we have is what we stand up in.[16]

For those Marines who had been interned in the Netherlands, time was to hang heavy on their hands in their hutted camp, known as 'Timbertown.' The days turned to months, and months to years. Some turned to handicrafts, making wooden jewellery boxes. For others, football was their chief occupation, and international matches were held between British and Dutch teams. The pay in the camp was poor, and the men could easily spend it all on the day that they received it on chocolates and other treats to enliven their days. Perhaps the only consolation was the invariable kindness of the Dutch people towards them, in contrast to the treatment meted out to many of those held in German hands. There was however a strong sense of frustration among many of these professional soldiers that they were idling their time away uselessly, whilst their country so obviously needed them. Private Benjamin Brooks of Glossop in Derbyshire was a long-serving Royal Fleet Reservist and veteran of the 1900 China campaign, who had been serving with the Plymouth Battalion of the Royal Marines at Antwerp. He wrote from the 'Interned Depot', Groningen Camp, Holland, on 19 December 1914, to a well-wisher at home. He and his comrades had clearly heard about the German navy's bombardment of Hartlepool and other towns on the North Sea coast, which had claimed the lives of women and children:

Dear Mrs Partington, please allow me to thank you and the people of my dear old town for the kind wishes and beautiful Christmas gift I received to-day. I can assure you that the boys in the Navy, and those who are fighting at the front, will appreciate it as I do. I know from bitter experience that the thoughts of the men just before going into action are for the loved ones at home, and it strengthens their aim when they know how you are thinking of them. We are all excited here over the awful outrage on our coast, and we hope something will happen so that we can get away and strike one more blow for our dear country. The boys here are all fighting fit again after their exertions in Belgium and around Antwerp, and it feels very hard to be caged up like this. But I am sure that the boys in and our gallant Navy, of which I am proud to belong and to serve, will strike the final blow to this hated German power.[17]

Not everyone who passed into Holland was interned however. Some thirty members of the band of the Royal Marines, who had been right through the siege and bombardment of Antwerp, arrived at Charing Cross railway station, to be met by a representative of the Press Association who was keen to know more about the circumstances of their escape. The bandsmen were clad chiefly in the caps and great coats of Belgian soldiers. One of them explained: 'We lost our own clothes, and these were the best substitutes we could get.' Another member of the party elaborated upon how they avoided being interned along with so many of their erstwhile comrades: 'we are bandsmen in time of

Two Royal Marines, one obviously wounded, on the retreat from Antwerp, 1914. (*Author's Collection*)

peace, but in war time we become Red Cross men, and it was as Red Cross men that we were in the trenches at Antwerp. When we evacuated the trenches we went into Dutch territory, with the rest of the British force that is there, but, as we were non-combatants, we were allowed through, and so were able get home again.' The terrible effect of the fire of the great German siege guns was mentioned by a third man, who remarked: 'Antwerp is in ruins. Buildings went down like a pack of cards under the terrific fire of the big guns. Our Marines and Naval Brigade fought well, but they did not get a chance to do much. It was chiefly an artillery fight, and our men had to keep steady under awful fire. It was a frightful experience. The German firing was very accurate, and the screech of shrapnel was nerve shattering. The casualties were not heavy. Our men were wonderfully cool, and the last few days their losses were inconsiderable.' Another of the arrivals said: 'It was the German artillery that took Antwerp. It was vastly superior to that of the Belgians. We went into the Belgian forts, and their guns did not seem to be as big our six-inch guns.'[18]

Another who made it home safely was Sergeant Arthur G. King, of the Royal Marine Light Infantry who was also a reservist. In a letter to his wife who resided at 79 Florence Road, Southall he gave a vivid account of the fighting he took part in:

> I expect you are wondering if I am in the land of the living or not, as I have not had the chance to write lately. It is sheer luck that I am alive, I can assure you. We have properly been 'through the mill' this week at Antwerp. I have seen any amount of my chums blown to bits. Poor old Tom was one of these I think he is the only one you would know. We were under a heavy shrapnel fire from last Sunday morning till Thursday night, and it was awful. The trenches were blown about our ears, and I was buried in earth for some time. If we had British artillery with us last Sunday we could have prevented the fall of Antwerp, as we were actually holding them back with our rifles only all that time. Us Marines and Belgians were the only troops there, and, of course, we had to retire, as it was too hot for us. The Germans' musketry is rotten, but their excellent artillery practice makes up for this deficiency.

However, I had the satisfaction of knocking five over in their tracks. But we have lost a fearful lot of men. Last Sunday and Wednesday was like 'Hell with the lid off'. We had to rush from Mortzel right through Antwerp during a heavy bombardment, the heaviest the world has ever known, about five shells a minute; broken glass, wood, and stone were flying in all directions, and the place was in ruins and flames. The skirt of my great coat is in shreds, my rifle had a piece knocked out of it, and yet I am still whole and well, but 'blooming' hungry. I have heard just now that we are to come home to reorganise; if so, I will try to come and see you. All our spare kit and a mail for us was blown up in Antwerp. I have had the same clothes on for about three weeks, and I don't feel very comfortable, I can tell you. It is a pitiful sight to see these refugees all leaving their nice homes to come to England. Every English family should take one in when possible. Have not had my clothes or boots off for three weeks, and shall enjoy a bath. Have just heard we leave for England to-night.

[On the outside of the envelope that contained this letter Sergeant King had written: *Have arrived at Deal since writing.*][19]

Royal Marines in Groningen internment Camp, 1914, following the fall of Antwerp. (*Pat Gariepy*)

A 19-year-old private of the Royal Marines, from Branstone near Burton-upon-Trent named William Hugh Topliss, was also among the large number of men who arrived at Deal after the fighting at Antwerp. He wrote an interesting letter to his grandparents, Mr and Mrs Goldsmith, of South Oak Street, in which he told them:

> We have been fighting at Antwerp and have lost about 800 men – 72 killed, 100 wounded, and the others taken prisoner. A trainload of our men were captured by the Germans when we were retiring. We arrived there with only our rifles, while the Germans had some very big guns and dropped shells in our trenches. As soon as we got in our trenches the Germans found the range and 'blowed' us up. They say that a Belgian general gave our position away, but he was caught and shot. We retired 25 miles one night, marching from eight p.m. until eight o'clock the next morning. We have had a terrible time, but have got through it alright, and I am surprised to find myself still alive. We have lost all our clothes, except those we stand up in and we have had no money for over a month.[20]

Private G. Thomas, Royal Marine Light Infantry wrote to his father at Tynemouth:

> We had a hard time in Antwerp. From the first we were suspicious of some of the 'Belgian' officers, who were wandering around with apparently nothing to do but watch us. Two of them attracted suspicion, and were found to be German spies. They were court-martialled and shot next day. You have probably seen a lot in the papers about the blunder of sending us there. My opinion is that it was no blunder at all, for there isn't the doubt that we did put life into the Belgian garrison, and if we only delayed the fall of the city by half an hour, that counts for a lot in this war. It was fine to see the way our boys took it. They lay in the trenches for eighty hours, and cracked jokes amid the terrible shell fire. Young Mr. Asquith, the Prime Minister's son, was as daring as anybody. He moved about giving us a cheery word from time to time, and nothing ever seemed to tire him. He had one or two narrow shaves, but bless he

never troubled about that. 'Wait and see' was his motto when the shells began to fly around, and be looked as if he wasn't going to worry until one hit. Officers like him make a lot of difference to men, and there isn't one of us that would not go through fire and water for him.[21]

As Thomas indicated, the Antwerp expedition was controversial at the time and has remained so ever since. To many it seemed like a disastrous failure, but Churchill, its architect thought it worthwhile. His strongly held view was that but for the resistance offered at Antwerp, and for the measures taken to prolong that resistance, the considerable enemy forces engaged would have been free to carry out an almost uninterrupted march upon the Channel ports. He believed that had the German siege army been released on 5 October to advance at once, nothing could have saved Dunkirk, nor perhaps Calais and Boulogne. The loss of Dunkirk was a certainty, and that of the latter two ports a probability. Apart from anything else the capture of these vital supply ports would have been a disaster for the BEF. Ten days' delay to the Germans was all that was needed to get British troops into Belgium from the Aisne, and those ten days were nobly won by the Royal Naval Division, including a high proportion of Marines. This achievement however belies the fact that the mobilization of the Royal Marine Brigade – to fulfil a role which might easily have been foreseen by the authorities before the outbreak of war – was a makeshift affair, bolstered by reservists who were really too old to fight well for an extended time, with a high proportion of half-trained young officers and recruits also among its ranks.

Musician Stanley Billings, Royal Marines Band. At Antwerp he served with the Headquarters of the RND, and died of Enteric Fever in 1915 whilst attached to Drake battalion RNVR. (*Author's Collection*)

Chapter Two

Gallipoli and the Dardanelles 1915

The Gallipoli campaign of 1915 must rank as one of the most ambitious, and at the same time most mishandled operations of the First World War. On paper, Churchill's plan to force the passage of the Dardanelles strait in the eastern Aegean had the potential in one fell swoop to both knock the Ottoman Empire out of the war, and to open up a southern route to Russia through the Black Sea. This would allow her to export much needed grain to Britain, and at the same time for the Western allies to keep her supplied with munitions. However, the failure by Churchill to heed expert advice (principally that the guns of British capital ships were not designed to neutralise shore batteries, and that the strait was heavily defended by minefields) meant that the army was only thrown in to try to capture the Gallipoli peninsula after the Royal Navy had already failed, and after all hope of achieving tactical advantage through surprise had vanished. Never the less the Marines of the Royal Naval Division, though now consisting largely of wartime volunteers, fought bravely from the beginning of the land campaign to the very end.

Private Wilfred Wheatley Cooper, in transit to the Dardanelles with A Company of the Portsmouth Battalion Royal Marines was typical of the newly enlisted wartime recruits, identified by the letter S after their service numbers, which Cooper described in a letter home as the Special Service Force (in fact, Royal Marine records confirm that the S stood for Short Service). His letter continued, describing the difficulties of obtaining 'comforts' in the Eastern Mediterranean, and referring to the naval bombardment of the Dardanelles; to him and probably most others it was obvious that a landing must be imminent:

> Having noticed that you are sending tobacco and cigarettes to the Derbyshire men serving their country, we hope to receive some. We

are not in France, but have seen more than some men out there. All the boys of Chesterfield here are unable to get cigarettes or tobacco. I give a list of them: Lance-Sergt. Cox, G. Jaggers, Buxton, S. Woolley, H. Thompson, K. Buckland, G. Whileman, J. Rogers, J. Holmes and F. Allison. Cigarettes sent to us c/o G.P.O. London, will be thankfully received and distributed amongst the above. Owing to the scarcity of writing paper we are unable to write home, and beg of you to put this letter in your columns and so oblige the pit lads. We are all first-class, but should be glad if we could get your paper just to see how things are going. We shall soon be going along the promenade as we call it, or the place that has been stopping the pills of Sir John Jellicoe's men, and when the time comes our Brigade will do just the reverse to what it did at Antwerp. Geo. Jaggers is in the machine gun section. I have found the place where women do the work and the men do nothing at all. My first aid packet and lint and bandage was made at Robinson and Sons, Brampton, and bears the date September, 1914 P.S.—Have the rest of the local boxers enlisted and followed the steps of T. Mitchell and the 8-stone champion? I hope so.

Being a pigeon fancier, Private Cooper added: 'I hear that it is doubtful as to whether they will allow any pigeon racing this season. I have found this life all right, and shall able to tell you something when we have given the 'knock-out.' Our opponents are breathing heavy now. This is my 5th week on the briny.'[1]

Two Royal Naval Division battalions were attached to the 29th Division for the initial landings at Gallipoli on 25 April 1915; Plymouth Battalion RMLI and Anson Battalion. They formed part of a force of 2,000 men who had landed at 'Y' Beach by 05.45 am: the other units being the 1st Battalion King's Own Scottish Borderers (KOSB) and the 4th Company of the South Wales Borderers (SWB). The force was led by the commander of the Plymouth Battalion, Lieutenant Colonel Godfrey Matthews, though this was disputed by the commanding officer of the KOSB, and a furious argument between the two, in full view of the men, was only ended when a piece of shell killed the latter officer. Although there was initially little resistance met at 'Y' Beach, no orders were initially received to press inland; eventually, after Turkish resistance had stiffened, the force was withdrawn. The remainder of the South Wales Borderers landed at 'S' Beach, their deficiency of one company being made up by the Marines of HMS *Cornwallis* who landed alongside them. Here again, despite weak Turkish opposition, little progress was made.

The rest of the Royal Marine Brigade did not take part in the first day landings of 25 April and was instead detailed to take part in a dummy landing in the Gulf of Saros, a feint designed to draw the attention of the Turkish defenders away from the true landings. The men were ordered to make as much noise as possible in disembarking, but the Turks did not take the bait and the brigade was soon re-embarked. By 28 April, the physical exhaustion of the 1st Australian Division at Anzac Cove was evident, and Sir Ian Hamilton had agreed to assign four battalions of the RND returning from their diversionary duties at Bulair to hold the line, while Australian General Birdwood's units reorganised and got a little desperately needed rest. The Anzacs, always confident in their own manhood, decried the physical immaturity and callow state of the marines, who were largely speaking wartime recruits, and by no means the finished article as soldiers. These men were to face a severe challenge when they began to take over the line between Courtney's Post and across 400 Plateau on the night of 28 April. In the pitch dark, with heavy rain adding to the difficulty, and contradictory orders seemingly shouted from all sides, they scrambled up the near vertical scrubby hillside and took over trenches that were often still choked with the dead and wounded:

> What confusion! Everyone shouting orders or asking for this or that battalion. Our Battalion waited for a guide to conduct them to the trenches. It was now pouring with rain. At last we commenced to move up in pitch darkness. The wounded were coming down on stretchers in a continuous stream. It was hard work scrambling up this hill in dense scrub. We were utterly worn out ... No one knew exactly where we were wanted or how to get there. It was a hard climb our hands were torn with the scrub. We arrived below the crest of the hill at 8pm. Orders came back to me that I was to remain where I was, the trenches were so full of dead and wounded that it would be difficult to move. I must have dozed off to be awakened

A Turkish artillery battery at Gallipoli. (*Library of Congress*)

by the voice of an Australian sergeant shouting, 'Give them a good 3 feet!' I looked up and saw them dragging dead Australians over the crest and burying them close by where we were lying.'[2]

Thus remembered former Private Harry Baker of the Chatham Battalion, Royal Marine Light Infantry. During the war, his parents Mr and Mrs Baker, of Brook Street, Aston Clinton, received a letter from him, aboard HM Hospital Ship *Letitia*, in which he related the dramatic experiences he had had with the Turks in this action:

We have been busy with the Turks, and have given them a hot time. Our Battalion has done very well. Edgar was unhurt when I last saw him; but poor old Charlie was killed on Friday, April 30. On

May 3 we went up to dig some trenches on a ridge just captured by the Australians, but instead of using our picks and shovels we had to use our rifles. The Turks were trying to re-capture the ground. About 50 of us managed to reach the top of the steep bank, and commenced to reply to their fire. There were eight other men with me, and suddenly a machine gun enfiladed us, and killed seven men and wounded me in the right foot. That left only one man (an Australian) untouched out of the nine of us, but few minutes after he was hit three times in succession, and never spoke again. The Turks did not get the ridge, as reinforcements came in time. I rode from the firing line to the beach on a donkey, and I think that the poor thing ought to have a V.C. for carrying my 12st. as it did. Please don't worry about me, as I am getting on fine, and can assure you we are well treated.[3]

In fact, the Victoria Cross was awarded to a Marine for this action. Lance Corporal Walter Parker, of Stapleford, Nottinghamshire was serving with the Portsmouth Battalion. Parker remembered later:

We were in and out, both night and day, attending to the wounded, and rendering first-aid to the injured. Having been at work in the Hospital some time, Col. Luard, Capt. Syson, and Capt. Morton came in quietly and called for a volunteer to go down to one of our own companies which was enfiladed. All of us realised the task was almost super-human.[4]

Lance Corporal Parker was the senior NCO on duty. To leave the company amongst which were many men wounded, and probably dying for lack of medical assistance, was a terrible thought. As no volunteers were forthcoming, Parker himself undertook to go. When he reached the frontline he began to work his way from trench to trench for some considerable distance, when he was suddenly confronted and threatened by an Australian officer who ordered him to abandon such a reckless mission. Regardless of this, he proceeded on his journey. To reach his goal he had to traverse an open passage, upon which, day and night, Turkish machine guns were constantly firing. The gallant Marine ran through this deadly trap, and, continuing down the hill into a place called the Valley of Death, fell into a pond at the bottom. The next thing which he became aware of was the tremendous cheering of the officers and men of his battalion, which was still under fire. He was the first man to go down and render them assistance, using every bandage and other equipment with which he had set out, so that he was left with none to dress his own wounds. He stayed with these troops throughout the night.

Lieutenant Bernard Henry Herford, Chatham Battalion, died of wounds on 2 May 1915. (*Author's Collection*)

The following account of the heroism of the Royal Marines in this spell of fighting was been written by an officer of the corps who had been invalided home, who had served for twenty-one years in the ranks, and on being called up at the outbreak of war was given a temporary commission in his old corps.

The history of the Royal Marines contains few episodes more striking or more dramatic than those which took place during the dramatic days of the landing of the British Mediterranean Expeditionary Force in the months of March and April, 1915. They are surely among the most brilliant achievements of British arms in all the glorious history of this country. After the first attack the Marine Brigade was ordered to support the Australians who had already 'made good' and were being heavily pressed at Gaba Tepe. Never shall I forget the thrill of pride as I once again saw the fine old corps, in which my grandfather and great-grandfather served and fought, parading for what proved to be one of the greatest efforts they had ever been called upon to make for God, King, and country. Veterans of many fights in various parts of our wide flung Empire stood shoulder to shoulder with clean-limbed lads of only a few months service, all of them alert and keen to tackle the job in hand, so much so that a young officer, turning to me, remarked, 'By Jove, one wouldn't think we were going into one of the bloodiest fights in history; just look at them, aren't they great?' And truly they were.

The outstanding features of this landing must remain indelibly printed upon my memory for all time. Those weird gullies lying between overhanging craggy hills, which in some places rose to a height of 200 feet, covered with thick, green foliage, varied here and there by patches of sand. Here is a party of men, working like Trojans, digging themselves in; yonder the Turkish trenches, illuminated with a myriad darts of flame, from each one of which speeds forth that messenger who calls men home. Fire crosses fire at point blank range. Turk and Briton have at length met in deadly grip to settle once and for all that long bid for sovereignty of the Cross over the Crescent. Rifle, bayonet, spade and pick axe, these are the tools by which that sovereignty is to be forged. The scene was awful in its grandeur, yet God-like in sacrifice, and I, who am privileged to write this record, bear witness to the fact, for have I not seen our men glorious in battle, patient in suffering. and splendid in death. Here is just one instance: A young officer is brought down to the dressing station, badly hit. His only anxiety is expressed in the broken utterance: 'How long will it be before I ran get back to my Boys?' Poor lad! He never went back. Another occurs to me. A young private, who had been shot through the leg, actually broke away from the clearing

PLY16802 Pte J.J.Maher, Plymouth Battalion, Royal Marine Light Infantry. After service at Antwerp, he went on to see action at Gallipoli where he was killed on 3 May 1915. He was from Dublin. (*Author's Collection*)

hospital, and by begging lifts in waggons he at last limped back to his comrades, with the single remark, 'I couldn't stick it back there with you boys at the front.' I am not romancing or writing for effect, I merely state here those things which I hope I may never forget ....[5]

Some months later, Private Fred Shaw, of the Chatham Battalion Royal Marines, wrote to his mother, who was living at the Bull's Head Hotel, Winsford, describing what had occurred since the landing at Gallipoli. He was surprisingly candid, and after stating that he was 'in the pink', he went on to say:

I suppose you read in the papers about the Australians and New Zealanders at Kaba Tepe [*sic*]. My word, it was magnificent! The country here is extremely difficult for a landing force, and the way they accomplished it was by jumping from the boats with just a rifle and bayonet – no ammunition, and charging up the cliffs through the enemy over the second ridge, and to the third, where they established themselves. Their losses were very heavy, though. We joined up with them two days later; it was raining hard, and that made things uncomfortable. Our introduction was to climb a hill 900 feet high, and then start straight away 'hammer and tongs.' The enemy tried several times to drive us out of the improvised trench, but we hung on to our position like grim death and inflicted great loss on the enemy; but the next afternoon they came on in overwhelming numbers and by sheer weight absolutely 'humped' us out of our front trench. (This was where the 'ham knife' came in handy!) Another company of our fellows reinforced us, along with several Australians, and we went for them 'bald-headed.' They yelled out 'Allah,' but to no purpose.... Out of the trench they scooted, and several of our fellows, rather excited, followed, only to bowled over by machine gun fire. The fighting continued throughout the night, attacks and counter-attacks being the order of things. Next morning, at daybreak, the sight that met our eyes was terrible, our dead and wounded being mixed with the enemy. We had to crawl out and drag them in one a time. This was a very ticklish job, as their snipers were rather hot on anything that moved. Eventually we got all our wounded in, leaving the dead until the cover of night should come to mask our movements. I cannot say too much for the valour of the Colonial troops: They are splendid. Ye gods! I would like to see 1000 of the mad Kaiser's famous Prussian Guards opposed to 500 of our half-trained Australians and New Zealanders. I'll bet he would say something stronger than Potsdammit at the result of the encounter! We spent eleven days in company with them, when to our mutual sorrow we had to leave. We came to Cape Hellas [sic] where we have been fighting off and on ever since. I thought Antwerp was bad, but this show knocks it into a cocked hat for 'scrapping.' We have been actually under fire for nearly four months; there's no such thing as back to billets here. We live a troglodytic life when not actually in the trenches – burrowed in the earth like so many rabbits – but not as you see them in the illustrated papers, with front and back doors and pictures on the walls. I expect those photographs are taken at a base camp somewhere, miles away from any firing.

The great discomfort here are the flies – millions of them. These are easily explained. Our friends on the other side seldom bury their dead; they invariably scatter a thin covering of earth over them, hence the countless flies. In scores of cases where we have taken trenches from them the parapets have been built up from bodies covered with sandbags and loose earth. I'll leave you to imagine the awful stench from the decomposing flesh; it would turn a skunk sick. A word or two about the Turk. He's a very game fighter, in fact he's twice as game as the German. If you corner him, stand by for a good set-to; there's no 'hands-up' with him, and if he has half a chance of beating you, he'll chance his luck and pin his faith in Allah. At the same time I think they are about sick of the whole business, and according to the yarns from prisoners we have captured, they are only held together by German officialdom, and the fact that they are fighting for their existence as a European power; but they'll have to 'get out and get under,' no matter how long it takes to do the trick.[6]

As the struggle for control of the peninsula continued, Private Horace Bruckshaw of the Plymouth Battalion recorded in his diary for 9 May:

Spent a rotten night of it, this is a terrible place simply infested with snipers. Nine of us went out with Capt. Andrews hunting them during the morning. Could find nothing however although we were sniped at every step we took. Luckily we all got safely back to our trench. Chapman wounded in chest this morning just as he got up to go to the assistance of another wounded man. It made us a wee bit nervous as he was sitting against me. After dark we went over the back of the trench to a point about a mile back to fetch rations up. We had just returned when the Turks greeted us with a fusillade of rapid fire. This they kept up all night.

One of the casualties here was Second Lieutenant Cecil J.T. Black, Portsmouth Battalion Royal Marines, the youngest son of Mr Wm. Black, JP, High Sheriff of County Monaghan, Ireland, who was killed in action at the Dardanelles on 9 May 1915. Second Lieutenant Black, who was only eighteen years of age, was educated at Trinity College, Dublin, and obtained his commission in the Royal Marines in August 1914, passing the examination at the first attempt. Shortly before the arrival of the telegram announcing his son's death, Mr Black had received a letter from the young officer describing scenes in the Dardanelles and informing his family that he was quite well. The announcement of Second Lieutenant Black's death was received with deep regret in the county of Monaghan. His elder brother, Thomas, was serving in the Royal Dublin Fusiliers. Bruckshaw continues:

Monday 10 May
Things went quieter by breakfast time but the snipers kept very busy. We laid pretty low all day. We have lost nearly all our officers with these blessed snipers. Captain Tetley is the latest victim having been hit in both legs while leading a party sniper hunting. Very few of them got back again. Heavy firing commenced at dusk and continued all night.

Tues 11 May
Getting our full share of casualties. Poor Capt. Andrews killed by a sniper just after dinner. We have lost our best friend. We have

only about five officers left. We are to be relieved today sometime. Left the trenches after dark and made our way back to some open ground about a mile and a half back. We had to doss down in the open. To make things worse it started raining.

Wed 12 May
It poured with rain all night but we were tired out and slept through it all. We got some breakfast and then made ourselves as comfortable as we could in some vacated trenches waiting for further orders. We buried Captain Andrews this morning together with Lieut. Barnes. The Colonel read the service and was very much cut up. The poor Captain's men felt it very much, most of us turning away before the service was finished. A mound, a small wooden cross and a few pebbles alone mark the last resting place of as brave a gentleman as ever walked. In the afternoon we moved further back and dug rest trenches for ourselves. Sir Ian Hamilton paid us a visit and complimented Col. Matthews on the work he and his men had done.[7]

The grave of Captain C.B. Andrews of No. 4 Company was later lost, and he is now commemorated on the Helles Memorial to the missing. He had returned from Australia to rejoin his old corps. He was killed when the Turks mounted a counter-attack on the French and the Naval Battalions, and for a short time the situation here was critical, but the situation was restored in front of the Marines positions by Captain Tetley RMLI who counter-attacked with No. 1 Company, Plymouth, as the enemy were on the point of breaking through, and threw them back. Lieutenant Jack Clixby Barnes, also killed during the attack, is likewise commemorated on the Helles Memorial. Little is known of his biography.

On 12 May the Plymouth Battalion was withdrawn to the rest camp behind the lines. This however should not be thought of as the equivalent of a rest camp in France. At Gallipoli nowhere was safe from enemy fire, and men were as likely to be hit by a bullet in the bivouac lines as at the front. Another short service Marine, Private Bertram Potts, this time of the Chatham Battalion was wounded at this time and it seems likely that this was by a stray bullet whilst on rest. Confirmation of the fact that he had been evacuated from the Peninsula came in the form of a letter written

Gallipoli and the Dardanelles 1915   37

to his brother at home. Private Potts was the son of Mr and Mrs J. Potts of Aldercar Lodge, Langley Mill, with whom much local sympathy was felt, and the news that his injuries were not so serious gave them a great sense of relief. An extract from the letter sent by Potts reads:

> [Just] a line to say I am going alright. Have about got over wound, but my leg is very weak. We had very hot time at the Dardanelles I can tell you. We landed the 28th of April, and I lasted until the 16th May, when I got a bullet in my right knee. Have still got the bullet in, and don't know whether they are going to take it out. Sid (meaning his companion, Sid Weston, the Heanor amateur weight lifting champion) was not wounded, but had to come away ill. I think he has gone back now. I am out camping but still in Egypt by the seaside, and it is very hot here. Send the Ripley and Heanor News I have seen another man here who used to drive the mineral water motor lorry for the Co-operative Society and lived in Dean-Street.[8]

One of the most unusual experiences was that of the author Compton Mackenzie, later known for his best selling novel *Whisky Galore*, who was commissioned into the Royal Marines in 1915. He wrote a semi-autobiographical account of his war experiences, entitled *Gallipoli Memories*. Ordered by Sir Ian Hamilton to report to the headquarters of the Mediterranean Expeditionary Force, he arrived in Alexandria only to discover that no one could tell him how to proceed to Gallipoli. He reported to the base commandant in the city but:

> He seemed to think I was an itinerant impostor. I produced Eddie Marsh's telegram which, with an expression of profound disgust he read through.
> 'Who is the fellow who signs this?'
> 'Mr Winston Churchill's private secretary.'
> The major snorted impatiently.
> 'I never heard of him. I don't recognise an irregular document like this. What is it?'
> 'It's an Italian telegram.'
> 'It may or may not be. Anyway, I can't do anything about it.'

I began to get a little irritated.

'Well, perhaps you will be good enough to telegraph G.H.Q. and get them to confirm these orders?'

'Why should I communicate with GHQ? I don't recognise this telegram as orders from anybody. I don't know who you are.'

'Well, can I telegraph to Sir Ian Hamilton myself?'

'No, you can't.'

'Then I am to remain indefinitely in Alexandria?'

'I don't care where you remain.'

'Can you give me an idea how long I am likely to remain here?'

'I can't give you the least idea of anything. It may be for two months, it may be forever.'⁹

It was an inauspicious start to a military career, and Mackenzie was afraid that the Allies would be in Constantinople before he could even join them. When he eventually got to Gallipoli, nobody was able to find him anything to do, and he seems to have wandered about the Peninsula until he was given clerical work in an office on the steamer that served as G.H.Q. with Captain George Lloyd, who told him, 'All the odds and ends get pushed in here.' Later he was appointed an official war correspondent, and eventually became involved in intelligence work.

The author Lieutenant Compton Mackenzie served with the Royal Marines at Gallipoli. (*Public Domain*)

A third attempt was now about to be made to capture the strategically important village of Krithia. Reginald M. Gale was a Royal Marine signaller here, with the Royal Naval Division Engineers. The attack, on 4 June, was his first experience of war and he was attached to a French formation. He witnessed the assault by French Senegalese troops, and remembered:

The rifle fire from the Turks rose to an unbelievable intensity. There was no sound of individual shots; it was a sustained roar. Looking up one expected to see a curtain of bullets and one had the feeling that even a finger above the parapet would get hit. Then the men began to scramble over the parapet. My heart ached for them as it looked like certain death to be in the open. Almost immediately the first casualty dropped back in the trench. He was a large black man and both hands were clapped to his thigh and the blood was spurting through his fingers. My dominant feeling was one of surprise that his blood should look exactly like mine; what colour I expected it to be I cannot say. More and more wounded came in and made their way either alone or assisted to the rear. The medical arrangements were probably situated in the support line but I can only say that I saw none at all. More casualties tumbled back. Some died as they fell; some just lay where they fell and died soon; I cannot recall any able-bodied men returning. The heat and the flies beat down.[10]

Later that afternoon Gale took a wrong turn in a trench which led him to a different sector. He continued his journey but it was difficult to make progress because the floor was covered in wounded – at least one of them winced, fearing that he was going to be trodden on. Gale risked taking a look over the parapet and saw scores of khaki clad figures lying amongst the parched grass and barbed wire – members of the Royal Naval Division:

They lay about like dead leaves in autumn. These were the men who had travelled out on Ivernia with me; the tough-talking Tynesiders who had been vaccinated on board and, as I had seen for myself, had arms black and swollen. I have no doubt that many died with one arm more or less incapacitated.[11]

Compton Mackenzie returned to the Peninsula in the aftermath of this battle, and continued his memoir:

On Monday, the seventh of June, there was a chance of crossing again to Cape Helles [the southern point of the Gallipoli peninsula] in a destroyer. I welcomed an excuse to escape from the stifling atmosphere of the tent which had been full of blood-stained Turkish notebooks for the last two days, and asked leave to visit my Divisional Paymaster to discuss the problem of my pay and at the same time try for a batman. The atmosphere at Divisional Headquarters was gloomy in the extreme. I was not astonished when I heard details of what the Division had been through last Friday. The casualties had been very heavy. They thought that the French had let them down completely on the right. Patrick Shaw-Stewart was seen running along, waving his cane and shouting, 'Avancez! Avancez!' The Senegalese came out of their trenches, advanced seventeen yards, and then bolted back into them like so many gigantic black rabbits, after which nothing would persuade them to show themselves again. I suppose this was after the Colonial troops and Senegalese had been bombed out of the Haricot Redoubt which they had held for a time. There was no disposition to put any blame for the failure of the fourth of June on the General Staff. Any gibing was mostly directed at Maxwell's Peninsula Press [a trench newspaper] which had come out with a rosified account of our 'success', though of course it was recognized that a daily sheet of unmitigated gloom would hardly be worth printing and circulating. I was promised a batman; but the problem of my pay looked like being for ever insoluble, and I started to walk back.

Small shells kept dropping all round me, and it seemed inevitable that I should be hit presently. There is no doubt that the sensation of being shelled when alone is most infernally unpleasant. After walking about three-quarters of a mile I felt inclined to sit down and cry with exasperation because those Turkish gunners would not realize that I really was not worth so much expensive ammunition. I wanted to argue with them personally about the futility of war. It seemed so maddeningly stupid that men should behave as impersonally and unreasonably as nature. Over to the right I saw a clump of trees and, feeling I simply must somehow get a sensation of cover, I hurried across toward them at a diagonal jog-trot. I could not have made a more foolish move, because apparently there was a well by them at which mules were watered, and at regular intervals the enemy used to spray the clump with shrapnel. I must have come in for one of those antiseptic douches, for the air was alive.

I began to worry about the proofs of [my novel] Guy and Pauline, thinking to myself that the printer's reader would be sure to change 'tralucent' to 'translucent' and that Secker [my publisher] in the depression caused by the news of my death would never remember how much importance I attached to getting rid of that unnecessary sibilant. Why couldn't those blasted Turks up on Achi Baba shut up? And I would have turned a gerund into a participle here and there … and probably there would be a vile nominativuspendens … at this moment I heard a burst of laughter and, looking round angrily, for I thought this laughter must be meant for the way I was definitely running by now, I saw a couple of men digging opposite to one another like the gravediggers in Hamlet and roaring with laughter every time one of the small shells either exploded or as often happened hit the ground with a thud and nothing else. Then one of the pair dropped. The other looked first at his pal and then at me who was hurrying past with haversack, water-bottle, pistol, and glasses jogging up and down in a most undignified way.

'Beg pardon, sir! Beg pardon!' he called out.

'You can't do anything,' I snapped. 'You'd better get into cover yourself as quickly as you can.'

'No, sir, it's not that', he whimpered as he cut across my path and forced me to stop while he saluted. 'But would you mind telling me if my friend's dead, sir, because I'm new at this job.'

'Of course, I'm not bloody well dead, you silly little cod', shouted the friend, who was sitting up by now and rubbing his head. And I left them, remembering another occasion when the friend actually had been killed and when the survivor's comment was, 'Beg pardon, sir, you think it's funny at first, but it's very serious really.'

By the time I reached the beach, the big gun on the Asiatic side of the Straits had started to shell the shipping. There were three preliminary fountains, after which a shell hit a French transport loaded with hay. The crew at once jumped overboard, and the transport caught fire. Then two destroyers rushed up and bundled all the men back on to their ship in order to extinguish the fire, which they succeeded in doing without being shelled any more.

I think it must have been that evening I met the last surviving officer of the Collingwood Battalion. He was very young, hardly more than eighteen and, after the horror of that experience to which he had gone almost within forty-eight hours of landing at Helles, he was being sent to do some work at Imbros in connection with the rest camp which was to be formed there. We did not talk about the battle, either then or at any other time. Oldfield was his name, and I hope he survived the battles in France later. I can hear now the tone of his voice as he said to me with a nervous little laugh:

'I'm the only officer left of the Collingwood.'[12]

Stores on the beach at Gallipoli. Tents in the background identify a 'rest camp'. (*Library of Congress*)

As trench warfare equally as vicious and deadly as any in France had set in on the peninsula, a cottage industry grew up in producing or adapting equipment suitable for this purpose. Trench periscopes and remote-firing rifles were two obvious examples of this, but the close proximity of the trenches led to makeshift 'factories' for jam-tin bombs and the construction of catapults, with which to fire them over 200 yards into the opposing positions. The jam tin bombs were made of gelignite, detonators and slow burning fuses, supplied from the RE stores on W Beach. The tin was filled with odd pieces of metal with would increase its deadly effectiveness in a confined space – old bullets and jagged fragments of Turkish shells were popular, according to Lieutenant (later Major General) Tom Jameson, whose Royal Marines company had been employed as divisional bombers. This unit had originally been the Cyclist Company of the Portsmouth Battalion, but Jameson recalled that when his men landed on the peninsula the cycles had been loaded into two barges. One drifted away and was never seen again. The other beached at Cape Helles, but there was little opportunity for cycling at Gallipoli.

In the newspapers of the Midlands, where many of the Short Service marines had been recruited, column after column reported on the fates of those who would not return from the Dardanelles. One such was Private Sydney Harrison who lost his life on 7 June 1915. His home was at 11 Canal Street, Ilkeston and he left a widow and two children to mourn his loss. At the outbreak of war he was a miner at Manor Colliery, Ilkeston. Having been formerly attached to the Territorial Force he volunteered again for service in September, in the Sherwood Foresters but after five days was drafted to the Royal Marine Light Infantry, Chatham Battalion. No details as to how he was killed have survived, but a communication dated 25 June 1915 was received by Private Harrison's wife from the record office of the Royal Naval Division:

> I deeply regret to inform you that telegram from Alexandria has been received to-day reporting that your husband, Private Sydney Harrison, R.M.L.I., who was serving with the Chatham Battalion, Royal Marine Brigade, Royal Naval Division, was killed in action near the Dardanelles June, 1915.[13]

Likewise much sympathy was extended to Mrs S. Hutchinson, of 25 Ratcliffe Gate, Mansfield on the death of her son. Private George Arthur Hutchinson, of the Royal Marine Light Infantry, was killed whilst in action in the Dardanelles, on 13 July 1915. The family received the official notification of his death two weeks later. Private Hutchinson was a millwright by trade, and his services were in great demand, as he was highly skilled in his work. Nevertheless, he enlisted in September 1914, and was stationed at Portsmouth for some time. He left one battalion of the Marines for another as it was his wish to get into action as soon as possible, and went out early in 1915.

PO-636 (S) Pte George Bird, Portsmouth Battalion RMLI, killed on 12 June 1915, he is buried at Redoubt Cemetery, Helles. (*Author's Collection*)

This time more details of the circumstances of his death were received, contained in a letter written by a comrade, Private John Herrod of the Chatham Battalion to friends at Mansfield. In it he said the Marines had had some hard fighting, and had been,

> …very sure of this job, but it does not seem as if the Turks will give us rest, so we shall have to keep plodding on. Geo. Hutchinson was killed in a charge the Marines made on the Turks. He got riddled with shrapnel and was killed on the spot.[14]

Sergeant Fred Shaw once again wrote a letter home, concerning this action; he pulled no punches about the brutality of war, but at the same time emphasised the ready sense of humour soldiers showed, even at the darkest of times:

> We made another advance on the 25th [May], this time without a casualty. The order was passed that 9pm we were to advance, and punctually to the hour we climbed over our parapet and wriggled or crawled until we came to the position we were told to entrench.

Everything was done so stealthily that the Turks were completely taken by surprise the next morning, when they found that the marines had dug themselves in right under their noses. They tried to drive us out, but the position was too strong for them; in fact it wasn't sport, it was murder shooting the poor devils as they tried to cross the open. The next forenoon a message was passed round from the G.O.C. and Generals commanding the divisions congratulating the Chatham battalion of Marines upon the splendid advance. The Turks tried another rush on July 6th, and allowed them come right to the trench; then we opened fire on them with rifles and machine gun. The result was appalling. The 75's of the French on our right simply mowed them down, and I don't think that out of the whole force that attacked in our sector more than 20 returned to their trenches. They lay about as thick as flies, not in dozens, but in hundreds. These were fresh troops who had only arrived the previous day from Adrianople, with the fixed intention of driving us into the sea. They couldn't have been pitted against a worse lot (for them) than either our brigade or the division the left. Both are old stagers, having been through the war from the beginning. Anyhow gave them a very warm reception.

The 12th of July was another red letter day for the Turks. We collared five lines of trenches from them, besides hundreds of prisoners. The fighting on both sides was very fierce. The last trench we took was awful. The bottom resembled a spring mattress, the reason being the bodies buried just below the surface. In lots of places arms, legs, and heads stuck through, the scant covering, the whole forming one of the most disgusting pictures imaginable. We couldn't live in this, so we dug another trench few yards in front. Of course we have some humorous episodes. A few days ago I heard a member of our sanitary squad rating a sentry for allowing paper to blow away from the incinerator, 'Nah then,' he said, 'what's the good of a bloke like you here; don't yer know that's what causes 'tripod' fever? I nearly rolled up with laughing. Another fellow, reading a general order from the medical officer as to refuse, etc., translated it thus: 'Now pay attention everybody! All bully beef tins, jam tins, bits of biscuit, etc., are to buried, as they cause fever – and it's to you keep it going – so don't forget to bury them by Col____ , and that's order!' Nearly everybody went into hysterics![15]

Perhaps the most moving account of a Marine killed in this action was that passed to Mr and Mrs P. Prince, of 217, High Lane, Burslem, who it was reported had received news of the death of their son, Private Albert Prince, a stretcher bearer in the Plymouth Battalion of the Royal Marine Brigade. The sad message was contained in a letter from the Reverend C.W.G. Moore, chaplain to the Royal Marine Brigade, of which the following is a transcript:

> Dear Mrs. Prince, no words of mine lessen the great loss you have sustained in the death in action of your noble son Albert. But I believe you will be glad to have some details concerning his death, which I am able to supply, and also to have the words which he dictated to me a few hours before he died. Surgeon Miller attended to him, and sent him at once to this ambulance, where I am now writing from. Albert was quite conscious and knew me. His wounds were again attended to, and he was placed in a shady shelter with 10 other abdominal cases, to lie quietly for 48 hours. But haemorrhage set in quickly, and his pulse gradually grew weaker. It was my privilege to stay with him for some time. The first thing he said to me was: 'I did wish to live for dear mother's sake, to look after her.' We prayed together, and then he asked if he might send a letter; so he dictated the enclosed, which speaks for itself. He said he was quite free from pain, and when he passed into the beyond, his face wore a serene look of rest and peace. We know something of your loss, for to the doctor and many officers and men in the battalion he was known and beloved. He has done splendid work on every occasion, and will be sorely missed. I buried him this morning, alongside of several comrades, in the little graveyard near this ambulance, about a mile from the firing line. Personally, I thank our heavenly Father for the witness of such self-sacrificing courage and such sublime faith. May our heavenly Father grant you His strength; and who can fail to gain strength when we see such lives, given by those who lovingly guided and used their influence aright, so that this time of

supreme trial has proved them ready and willing to give their dearest and best for the life of our beloved country, Empire and humanity. Pardon these few halting lines. Please accept my warmest sympathy with you and Mr. Prince, and believe me, yours sincerely, C. W. G. Moore, Chaplain Royal Marine Brigade.

The last letter of Private Prince to his mother, dictated in his dying moments to his chaplain, reads as follows:

'3rd East Lancs. Advance Field Ambulance July 14th 1915. My Dear Mother, I am writing now knowing that I am dying, but I thank God, knowing that I die right, doing my duty as a Briton should. I am very sorry that all my hopes and all my happy dreams I've had of living for you are lost. But do not worry, dear mother, for I shall meet you in the other land. Give my love to my father, brothers, and sisters. May God bless you and protect you, and may the cause for which I have died assist to bring success to our dear country. Good-bye, dear mother and all, for I must now close my eyes for good.—Your most affectionate son, Albert.' This was dictated to me, C. W. G. Moore, Chaplain. Royal Marine Brigade, by Private Albert Prince, stretcher bearer, Plymouth Battalion, Royal Marine Brigade.[16]

Private Prince was only 19 years of age when he left his employment at the Chatterley Whitfield Colliery and responded to the call of his country, in September 1914. He was well known to a wide circle of friends in Burslem.

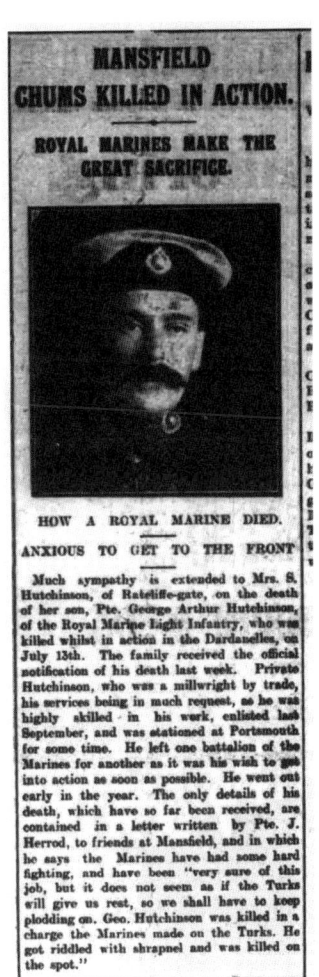

A cutting from the *Mansfield Reporter* carries news of the death of George Hutchinson. (*Author's Collection*)

He was Mentioned in Despatches for his heroism at Gallipoli, at the close of the campaign.

In this era, wounds to the lower abdomen were often fatal. Likewise, head injuries were seldom survivable, but in August Mr and Mrs Evans, of 49, Dingle Road, Higher Tranmere, received an extraordinary letter from their son, Private George Elliot Evans, of the Royal Marine Light Infantry who was hit during the recent fighting at the Dardanelles. He wrote:

> I am writing these few lines from a hospital ship where I am lying wounded. In the first place I must ask you not to worry at all, as the wound is not particularly severe. I was helping to repel an attack from the enemy, and caught a bullet in the head. The doctors tell me I am very lucky, as in 99 cases out of 100 a bullet in the head means instant death, so you see I have a lot to be thankful for. The ship I am on is like paradise compared to what I have been used to these past ten weeks. Everything is the acme of comfort, and I am waited on hand and foot; in fact, I can hardly realise where I am yet. I met a chap from Birkenhead when I was being carried from the trenches, and he was a real treat. Everything he could possibly do for me he did.[17]

PO18249 Pte Herbert Blades, from Nelson, Lancashire. He served ashore at Gallipoli in August 1915, before returning to sea service aboard HMS *Hindustan* and HMS *Cyclops II* at Scapa Flow. (*Author's Collection*)

Private Evans had joined the Cheshire Regiment at the outbreak of war but after four months' service was discharged as unfit. Determined to do his bit, he succeeded in joining the Royal Marines a month later, and his service record confirms that he received a 'Wounds and Hurts' certificate for a gunshot to the right side of the forehead at Gallipoli. He recovered and went on to serve in France, being wounded again before being discharged.

Reinforcements continued to arrive at the Dardanelles, but scarcely in sufficient numbers to make up for the heavy casualties sustained in June and July. In early August 1915 John Clegg (known as Jack) left for Gallipoli on the troopship *Royal George*. By mid-August Jack was in the firing line at Cape Helles and some of his letters from that time survive. He comments that the only additional food that the men could buy was eggs, and although he was part of the cyclist company he had only used his bike to ride down to the beach for a swim. Already Jack was feeling the effects of active service:

> I'll bet you'd find a difference in the smart, tidy marine who came home & the chap with a dirty & torn uniform & about a fortnights beard on.[18]

Clegg was born on 20 February 1896 in Dodworth near Barnsley, Yorkshire into a working class family. When the war broke out he was 18, and decided to join the Royal Marine Light Infantry in Manchester on 10 November 1914. Even though it was wartime, he chose not to sign on for Short Service but instead signed on for twelve years, which was the norm for regular recruits. Jack had spent time at the Marine depot at Deal in Kent for his basic training. For a regular marine the training lasted about a year and included artillery training for sea service as well as infantry training for land duty, although this was curtailed slightly due to the pressure of war.

Clegg quickly discovered that the climate and the flies were as much enemies as the Turks at Gallipoli. Both led to disease, and caused a steady drain in manpower. He was also losing weight rapidly and had swapped socks for some chocolate, presumably in order to try to gain strength. On 19 September Jack Clegg was evacuated from Gallipoli to Cairo with dysentery. In a letter, he informed his family that he was the ninth cyclist out of a platoon of ten to be evacuated in this way. Around this time, on 5 September, Surgeon David Revell Bedell-Sivright (known as

'Darkie') the Medical Officer of the Portsmouth Battalion also succumbed to disease. A friend recounted his death:

> I have seen a man who was with him nearly to the last. He tells me that Darkie had returned from a long spell in the trenches at an advanced dressing station, and came back properly fagged out. Some sort of insect bit him, and, being in a weak condition, poisoning set in, and he died two days later.[19]

He was a Rugby international, who had represented Scotland before the war, but his physical fitness had been steadily eroded by the conditions on the peninsula. Conditions in Egypt for men recovering from wounds or illness were a world away from those at the front, and excursions to historic sites were available. Councillor T. Williamson, the secretary of the Hoyland Silkstone Colliery, had received a letter from a former employee, Private A.C. Rawson, another of the Royal Marines recuperating in Egypt. In it he stated:

> I am sure that you do not get weather at home like we get it here. At Cairo it is about 80 degrees in the shade most days, but it is somewhat cooler where I am now billeted. Last Saturday I had a trip to the Pyramids and the Sphinx. I cannot describe my feelings whilst inside one of the largest of the Pyramids. One can only stand in wonder and the more one looks the more one wonders. On the Monday I paid a visit to the Museum, and there I saw the famous jewels, etc., which were found in the tombs at the Pyramids.[20]

CH-164 (S) Pte Thomas William Litchfield, Chatham Battalion, who served at Gallipoli until wounded on 1 October 1915. He later served aboard HMS *Prince George* and HMS *Inflexible*. (*Author's Collection*)

After recovery, Jack Clegg was transferred to Mustapha barracks at Alexandria, to await drafting back to Gallipoli. In a letter home he mentioned a rumour that convalescents were soon to return, and so drew pay that he was owed and spent it on expensive meals and carriage rides, things not normally an option for someone of his background. Clearly this was a type of fatalism – he knew he had a strong chance of not surviving a second tour of duty. So in late October, Jack was back on Gallipoli, now smoking a pipe in the naval tradition rather than the cigarettes he was used to. He was put on to labouring duties, and it appears that most returned dysentery patients we put onto digging work. The weather was getting cold, and thigh boots and mackintoshes were being issued. Food continued to be poor, and so anything contained in parcels from home was welcome, and Jack asked for Curry powder and cocoa so he could vary his diet. He asked for them to be packed in a tin, to avoid splitting. Early in November he reported that the weather was changing:

> It's dinner time & just beginning to rain. I hope it will clear up before night. I've only one waterproof sheet & I had a night out last week. My dugout was flooded & my blankets wet through.

The food though was apparently improving:

> We're allowed 1/3 of a two pound loaf of bread per day, which means about two ordinary slices. A rasher of bacon in the morning & Jam at tea time. However we can always get biscuits-which by the way are as hard as a bunker plate.[21]

At the end of 1915 Secretary of State for War Lord Kitchener visited the Gallipoli Peninsula to see the situation there for himself. At the end of his inspection, he recommended to the War Cabinet that the best course of action now was evacuation and redeployment of the troops involved. Churchill scathingly remarked that, 'he came, he saw, he capitulated.' It was a bitter pill to swallow for those who had suffered so much and who were now leaving behind only the graves of comrades to mark their sacrifices. Ironically, the evacuation was the most meticulously planned part of the eight month campaign and was achieved with minimal casualties. The Royal Marines were the last to leave Gallipoli, replacing both British and French troops in a neatly planned and executed withdrawal from the beaches. It even required some Marines to wear French uniforms as part of the deception. The diary of Sergeant Fred Shaw, sadly now lost, chronicled the daily doings of the Royal Marine Brigade. The diary concluded with the story of the evacuation on 7, 8 and 9 January 1916, which the writer described as 'the greatest bluff in history', adding:

> Twas not without some pang of regret that we left. It had been our home for over eight months. The regret was also for the thousands of gallant lives which had been lost – the cream of the Empire – fierce-looking Sikhs from the Punjaub [*sic*], laughing little Ghurkas from the hills of Nepal, sturdy Colonials from Australia and New Zealand, kilted men from over the 'border,' sons of toil from the Emerald Isle, miners from Wales, and men from every part of England, along with their brethren from France and her Colonies – all had paid the great price![22]

PO-899 (S) Pte George Frederick Barber of Leeds. He served with the Portsmouth Battalion of the Royal Marine Brigade at Gallipoli from 18 August 1915. He was killed in action on 27 November 1915. (*Author's Collection*)

After the evacuation the Marines were landed at Salonika and ultimately were transferred to France. The Gallipoli adventure had promised so much, but ultimately ended in bitter recrimination. So often the bravery and fortitude of the troops in the trenches, facing shells and bullets as deadly as any if France, as well as disease, poor food and bad weather, was accompanied by muddle, confusion and indecision by those at senior military and political level, in whose hands the ultimate direction of the campaign lay.

Chapter Three

Sea Service 1914–1918

When the First World War began, Britain's Royal Navy had already mobilised. The process was smooth and efficient and soon over 10,000 Marines were serving in ships at sea across the world's oceans. Aboard the largest ships, marine detachments were about half red and half blue marines. Light cruisers, however, had only red marines. The detachment commander, called the Officer Commanding Royal Marines, could be either of the artillery or light infantry. Thus the immediate task began of neutralising enemy assets wherever they were encountered. British crews were confident that the Royal Navy, the world's most powerful fleet, was more than capable of carrying out this task, and the mood generally was buoyant. Marines traditionally manned a portion of the ship's guns. In battleships, battlecruisers, and cruisers, the Royal Marine Artillery usually manned the main armament while the Royal Marine Light Infantry manned the secondary armament. Other duties of marines included providing guards and sentries and serving as officers' valets. Their most distinctive role was to serve as the backbone and spearhead of naval landing parties, a mission unchanged since the nineteenth century. Thus Marines saw action at Gallipoli, and the Battle of Jutland, but also in a host of smaller and less frequently reported operations.

Some saw action almost at once, in the Mediterranean in pursuit of the two major German warships there, the battlecruiser *Goeben* and the light cruiser *Breslau*. Lance Corporal Fred Morgan, Royal Marine Light Infantry, was serving aboard the armoured cruiser HMS *Warrior*. He was the son of Mr Thomas Morgan of Main Street, Bangor, Ireland and before he joined the navy about seven years previously, Lance Corporal Morgan had gained a scholarship in the Belfast Technical Institute for general subjects. Like his father, he was also a noted swimmer and diver, and about two years before the war he was recommended for the post of naval instructor in swimming at Devonport, by some officers who knew him. For some days previous to the declaration of war the British ships at Alexandria were keeping a watchful eye on these two powerful German ships. In a letter dated 9 August 1914 received by Mr Morgan from his son, he wrote:

> We are at sea between Greece and Malta, coaling from a collier, and she is taking this letter back with her. As yet no harm has befallen me or any of us here. We are waiting to see how Austria and Italy are going to place themselves. Only one ship here, a German ship called the Goeben, has more speed than our fleet. When she is put out of the way we will have little to fear from any.[1]

The *Goeben* and *Breslau* managed to escape from the still-neutral port of Messina on 10 August. When the news was transmitted to the British ships, the order was given at once, 'Clear for action.' The British ships which lay in waiting were all inferior to the *Goeben* in size, armament, and speed. As a precautionary measure against fire caused by a direct hit, every article of wood was thrown overboard, and amongst these was a valuable armchair belonging to the captain of the *Warrior*, on which was marked his name and also that of the ship. Thereby hangs a tale, for the crews of the British the ships were ready for action. The enemy ships were expected after nightfall, but just before they hove in sight the flagship signalled not to attack. Whatever had happened, it was a sad disappointment. The captain's armchair however was later picked up by a trawler, and taken to Fiume, the Hungarian port on the Adriatic. Here it was placed in the museum with a label attached, on which was printed: 'This is all that remains of the British cruiser *Warrior*.' The Austrian and German papers gave long accounts of the sinking of the ship, but a week or two afterwards she took part in the destruction of two Austrian cruisers and a torpedo boat in the Adriatic.

After the battle in the Adriatic, the *Warrior* sailed along the Palestine coast. South of Jaffa a force of Turks was located, and a party of marines and sailors were landed to engage them. The Turks were defeated, and 300 prisoners were taken. These were armed with rifles of the Mauser type and sword bayonets, one of which Lance Corporal Morgan brought home as a trophy. The sword bore a French maker's mark from the St Etienne arsenal, and date 1869. These were evidently used by the French in the Franco-Prussian war of 1870, and subsequently sold to the Turks. The captured enemy were taken to Ismailia, and imprisoned there. While waiting at Port Said to escort Indian troops, the whole of the 700 strong crew of the *Warrior* took part in a rifle shooting competition to determine the best shot in the ship, and after a severe test Lance Corporal Morgan came out on top. He added the badge for best marksman – crossed rifles, surrounded by a star and encircled by a floral wreath – to that which he already held for the most accurate distance finding. Morgan later sailed in much colder waters, the *Warrior*'s patrol work taking her north to the seas around Iceland.

Gunner John William Schofield of the Royal Marine Artillery Reserve was mobilised upon the outbreak of war and posted to HMS *Prince George*, a pre-dreadnought battleship which was on duty in the English Channel, escorting the BEF to France. He wrote a letter to his parents, Mr and Mrs Enoch Stansfield of Fence, Lancashire which was dated 24 September 1914. In it he gave his location as 'At Sea', and in the course of the letter he asked:

> What do you think of the splendid charge the Greys and Lancers at Mons? Wasn't that a beautiful and great game those boys played? I should long to get out there with our forces, but this game seems awfully tame. I thought were going to have a dust up when we put in at Ostend some time ago. I had a good look out for my old shipmate, John McKay, but there were that many 'Blues' there that it was almost impossible to look for him, and we had but very little time that would enable me to make the necessary enquiries. I guess he was somewhere in the great mob. Why we shoved off from that place I cannot say. I suppose the 'Heads' got well in the know of something that required seeing to elsewhere. Anyhow, we are still churning up the beautiful blue waters and looking out for things that have got a nasty cunning way of skylarking about below and putting a whole ship's company out of mess when they least expect it. One would not mind so much if there were some real good fighting to done, but when you meet with one those sneaking little devils and you don't

happen to get there first, it's case of up and under, and you don't get a look in at all. Rotten way of fighting, isn't it? ... We do not get too much sleep, for it's case of ever on the watch, but nothing doing. Would not mind in the least if there was something show at the finish. Hope to goodness we shall get a look in soon, and be able to do our bit in the firing line... I can't say where we are, somewhere on one of the ocean trade routes ... I have almost forgotten what it is like to be on shore. Eleven weeks come Monday since we mobilised this ship, and we have been on the run ever since.²

PO15801 Pte George William Walter, HMS *Good Hope*, killed in action 1 November 1914 at the Battle of Coronel. He was aged 20. (*Author's Collection*)

Other men were in action at the Heligoland Bight, and in September 1914, 200 lost their lives in the sinking of the British ships HMS *Cressy*, *Aboukir* and *Hogue* by enemy torpedo in the Broad Fourteens. In November almost the same number were killed aboard the *Good Hope* and *Monmouth*, overpowered by German Admiral von Spee at the Battle of Coronel. This defeat was avenged at the Battle of the Falkland Islands on 8 December. On this occasion, von Spee had attempted to raid Port Stanley without realising that a superior British naval force was refuelling there. Von Spee knew that, with his crew battle-weary and his ships outgunned, the outcome this time would be inevitable. Realising his danger too late, and having lost any chance to attack the British ships while they were at anchor, Spee and his squadron dashed for the open sea. The British left port around 10:00. Spee was ahead by 15 miles, with the German ships in line abreast heading southeast, but there was plenty of daylight left for the faster battlecruisers to catch up with them. As the battle progressed SMS *Nurnburg* was chased down by HMS *Kent*. During the engagement a German shell exploded against the gun port of the A3 casemate. The flash set fire to charges inside the casemate and the flames spread down the hoist and would have ignited a charge at the bottom, if it had not been flung out of harm's way by Sergeant Charles Mayes, Royal Marine Light Infantry, who then flooded the compartment. If the charge had ignited, the flames could have spread along the ammunition passage into the magazine and caused an explosion that would have blown the ship apart. Sergeant Mayes' presence of mind was recognised with the award of the Conspicuous Gallantry Medal.

Lance Sergeant Harry Wright, of the Royal Marines, sent to his sister, Mrs A. Hall, of Pumphouse Lane, Hanbury, a record of his experiences in West Africa around the same time. The letter was addressed from HMS *Cumberland*, a Monmouth class armoured cruiser, then at the mouth of the River Dualla, in the Cameroons, a German colonial possession. Dated 11 September 1914, it ran as follows:

Just a line to let you know that although I am hungry, thin, and weak, I am otherwise in the pink of condition. We are able to send a mail from Calabar, so I am writing on the off chance. We arrived in Victoria (German town) about a week or ten days ago. We landed in the afternoon (50 marines and a few sailors), but met with no opposition until 7.00 a.m. the following morning, when we were surrounded by German troops. A flag of truce was sent to us ordering us to leave German territory at once, or be attacked. Needless to say we did show our heels, and left in our boats, the Cumberland leaving after she had shelled the town from her 6 in. guns. During our stay at Victoria I was sent in charge of 12 men to a place called Botu, four miles from Victoria, with orders to prevent any trains leaving the station. Whilst there I nipped all the telegraph wires, broke into the station office, and smashed the cupboards open and took any papers and documents I thought valuable to prevent the trains leaving. I ordered the native drivers (with the aid of a loaded rifle) to take the fires from the engines. We had orders to treat the Germans with respect, but anyone coming to the station I searched for firearms. The station was situated in a cocoa plantation, and you could walk over oranges there also see the cocoa nuts growing on the trees. Whilst out at Bota I was in communication by signal with my captain, and I had to inform him what we were doing. We are now at the mouth of the Dualla River, about 20 miles from Dualla, the capital of the Cameroons. It will take us about ten days to get there owing to the shallowness of the river, and we have to sweep it for mines. They are sending wireless messages through saying they will give us a warm reception when we get there. Our own troops are marching from inland, and we are arranging to meet at the same time and work in co-operation with each other. In any case we shall have some fun. We (the Marines) have to land and search the riverbanks for hidden guns.[3]

Lance Sergeant Wright continued to send a commentary on his service in West Africa to the newspaper, and in his next letter he expressed the hope that this might go a little way towards helping recruiting in the various districts round Bromsgrove. He continued with a description of his service in a gunboat:

In my last letter, which I sent from Kribi, I mentioned that the Germans had attacked the defenceless town of Batanga and massacred the natives, taking possession of the town. The French Commandant decided to take a force of 150 men and surprise the Germans, H.M.S. Dwarf taking the force down by sea. I volunteered to go with them, and my services were accepted. Everything was kept secret, and we embarked in surf boats one dark night and paddled over to the Dwarf. During the night we weighed anchor and arrived off Great Batanga about 3.00 a.m., under cover of darkness. We now saw rockets being fired at Kribi, denoting the Germans were attacking, and recalling us back, but the place being very strongly fortified, the Commandant and Captain of the Dwarf decided to carry out the operation, so the bombardment commenced. Nearly all the houses were painted white, and made a beautiful target in the semi-darkness. Range was given to the gunners, and the shots took effect after the first two rounds. It was a glorious sight to stand there amidst the thunder of the guns and watch the shells throw up a red glare as they burst on their object, doing terrible damage to the houses and their effects, until nearly every house had been a target and demolished. After the bombardment the force embarked in the boats, and proceeded by the Dwarf's steamboat (with a maxim in the bows), we got near to the shore. The maxim having fired a sweeping fire into the bushes, we jumped out of the boats, and waded through the surf, lining a sandbank as soon as we got ashore. I signalled the Dwarf to let them know we had effected a safe landing, and were proceeding towards the town. Scouts were sent out, and we commenced to advance, but there was not a German to be seen anywhere; they had decamped, leaving everything behind.

We learned from an American missionary and natives that they had retired in the direction of Kribi, so we followed in that direction. Kribi was some 30 miles off. What a terrible mess our shells had made of the town. How fine it would be to take some of the shirkers at home and show them what could happen to an English town thanks to their un-patriotism. What a blessing the war is not in dear old England, where at present the old and infirm, the women and children, and our cripples and invalids, are perfectly safe. No one can understand without actual experience the misery caused by modern warfare, and with so much at stake it is a crime for any young man (without cause) to be comfortable at home. The Dwarf followed us in the direction of Kribi, and when we got to a clear open space I signalled informing her of the position of our troops. We met with no opposition at all thanks to the Germans not knowing how to carry out an ambush, which would be quite easy in so dense a country. We finally reached Kribi late that day, having covered thirty miles under a blazing hot sun, in full kit and 150 rounds of ammunition, the roads or tracks being only wide enough for one to walk along. Our comrades in Kribi gave us a hearty welcome, and informed us the Germans had made a fierce attack during our absence, but had been repulsed each time with losses. The Germans had taken advantage of our absence, and withdrawn their force from Datanga, and knowing Kribi would be weakened by our absence, had tried to re-take it, but failed.

No doubt their spies, of which there many among the natives, had informed them our departure. A French battle cruiser (Pothuan) now arrived at Kribi, and supplied her own signalmen, so we were recalled back to Duala, taking passage in the Dwarf. Most days we landed and marched into the country, starting early in the morning and getting back in the evening. We would cover anything from twenty to thirty miles, but a march out here is not to be compared with a march on the continent. Under a terrific hot sun, going in single file along narrow tracks, wading through swamps, pushing our way through dense undergrowth and creepers, cutting your arms, face, and knees (we wear shorts); millions of mosquitos to bite you as you walk along, and when we did come to a decent track it would be a sandy bottom. We had just got back from a long march one day when the Germans swooped down on a friendly native village, and killed seven of them, which goes to prove they used to watch our movements. We managed to surprise them once, and killed the Governor of Campo (a white man) and black soldiers by firing a volley into the bush. They replied to our fire, but our only casualty was one private who had the muscle of his arm shot away and the arm broken by a dum-dum. It is astonishing the quantity of fruit which grows out here. During our marches we would pass through cultivated plantations growing bananas, sugar cane, cocoa, jams, pan pans, breadfruit, prickly pears, pineapples, and lots of other fruits, all growing abundantly. We have very scanty news of what is taking place on the continent, but we have every faith in our troops fighting the greater battle, and much regret not being with them, but every little helps, and we hope to finish here soon and then come home, either to help our friends in France or wile away a few weary months up the North Sea. With every success to your paper and my friends in Bromsgrove.[4]

Other British assets were chasing down rogue German battleships such as the *Emden*, at large in the Pacific Ocean. Private B. Evans, of the Royal Marines, was at sea in these waters, and in a letter to his parents he related the details of a raid carried out against a coaling station in the German West Pacific colonies, at Yap, the administrative capital of the Western Caroline Islands, which had been purchased from Spain by Germany some years before. He stated:

We are just returning to Hong Kong, after having been to the Philippine Islands and the Fiji Islands. We destroyed a German possession called Yap, and bombarded all the ships in the harbour, burned all the coal in the coal yards, broke all the cables to America, and destroyed the wireless station. We properly gutted the place. On landing we were attacked by native police and troop of soldiers; but we soon got our rifles, maxims, and field guns to bear on them. Several of our chaps got killed, and we showed no mercy to our enemy and shot them at sight. We have got four women and baby and several Germans aboard here. We took them off a packet, which we sank about sixty miles from Yap. She had coal, provisions, ammunition, mines, and mails aboard for the German battleships. We are going to coal and provision, and then we are going to chase the battleships. We should have met them in the Fiji Islands, but it was false news we had.[5]

This Royal Marines recruiting poster shows members of the RMA manning a 6-inch gun. (*Library of Congress*)

In colder waters was Corporal George Finch who had been an errand boy, born in Devonport, when he first enlisted in the Royal Marine Light Infantry. From December 1914 to November 1915 he served aboard HMS *Oropesa*, a former ocean liner of the Pacific Steam Navigation Company, which like many of her ilk was armed and converted into an Auxiliary Cruiser. She was operating out of Liverpool on patrol duties, enforcing the blockade of Germany – tedious, unglamorous but necessary work. Finch described how on one occasion he saved the ship from a German submarine. He was later awarded the Distinguished Service Medal for this action, though no citation appears to have survived. He recalled:

I was the look-out man. We were going about 14 knots when I spotted the submarine's periscope. I reported to the bridge, 'Submarine off the port bow, sir'. I had a loud voice and everyone moved quickly. I saved the ship. We sank the submarine. If I hadn't shouted, we'd have had it.

Finch later rose to the rank of colour sergeant and ended his service with the Royal Marines Police. He added, 'I'm a serviceman through and through. I was a boy bugler when I joined the Navy in 1908.'[6]

It was a sad fact in this war (as in many others throughout history) that numerous casualties were to be sustained through accidents, and not enemy action, though it is frequently the case that such accidents are the combination of large amounts of high explosive and a wartime sense of fatalism sometimes bordering on carelessness. On 26 November 1914 the pre-dreadnought battleship HMS *Bulwark* was destroyed by an internal explosion, with the loss of 741 men, near Sheerness; only a dozen of her crew survived the detonation. It was probably caused by the overheating of cordite charges that had been placed adjacent to a boiler-room bulkhead. As there were only a handful of survivors, one of them, Sergeant John Budd of the Royal Marine Light Infantry gave evidence to the subsequent enquiry from his hospital bed. He was suffering from a broken leg and burns. He recounted how at ten minutes to eight he was finishing his breakfast on the port side of the second deck when he saw a sudden flash aft. He turned out at once and at the same instant the deck seemed to open and he was hurled into the water. He said he heard no explosion, but as he rose to the surface, he saw that the ship had gone. He was picked up by a service boat.

Similarly on 1 January 1915 the pre-dreadnaught battleship HMS *Formidable* was conducting training exercises in the English Channel. Despite the known risk of U-boats, no anti-submarine measures were in place, and she was torpedoed by U-24. In the long wait of over two hours in the darkness of a bitterly cold winter morning there was no panic. All the men were assembled quietly on the upper deck, many of them in the slightest of clothing. All portable woodwork was brought above, and part of one of the decks pulled up to provide more floatable material. It was generally thought that the ship would float until dawn, and while the rest of the crew were waiting on the upper deck, each with some woodwork at his side, the turret crews endeavoured in vain to correct, by shifting the position of the guns, the terrible list which the ship had developed. At the end of another three-quarters of an hour it was evident that she would not float much longer – in addition to the list she was sinking by the head. Still there was no departure from discipline. With the vessel nearly flat on her side in the last ten minutes, some hundreds of men had climbed over the rails on to the side which was out of the water, and stood there in two ranks waiting for the order to move. It came at last in the captain's words: 'Into the water with you, she's going!' and not until then did the men commit themselves to the darkness and the sea. One typical instance of individual heroism stands out among many others. Sixteen-year-old bugler Stanley C. Reed, of the Royal Marine Light Infantry, when he was advised to use his drum to keep himself afloat, replied that he had given it to one of the blue-jacket boys who seemed to have no very reliable support for the final plunge. This quiet little act of self-sacrifice – the bugler was not among the rescued – did not pass unnoticed. A Royal Humane Society bravery medal was sent to the boy's parents, as well as a letter from the Admiralty expressing their deep appreciation of the act.

British warships made up the major part of the Anglo-French fleet, which was assembled in the Aegean in early 1915 to attempt to force the passage of the Dardanelles. On the afternoon of 26 February, a destroyer towed in cutters from HMS *Irresistible* to the Seddel Bahr beach. Thirty sailors and forty-five Marines were in this party, and their task was to destroy the big guns in the fort and the torpedo tubes. The guns were destroyed with wet gun cotton, which had been broken up and made into 30lb charges in canvas bags about nine and a half inches in diameter (just less than the bore of the guns). These bags were fitted with canvas straps, so that they could be carried on the backs of the men, leaving the hands free for a rifle or other implement. A tin tube was contained in each bag for the insertion of a dry gun cotton primer. These were carried separately, and were fitted with two detonators, one for electrical and one for time-fuse firing. By use of these all six guns were put out of action, the first four being detonated simultaneously resulting in an enormous explosion, but the expected torpedo tubes could not be found.

A landing party of British troops coming ashore at Kum Kale, Gallipoli. (*Library of Congress*)

Other parties were sent to Kum Kale, where the enemy gunners fled, and under a covering guard of the Royal Marines of HMS *Vengeance*, the sailors had gone from gun to gun and then taken cover as each gun was destroyed by individual charges. Midshipman William-Powlett, aboard the ship, recorded the progress of the demolition party here in his diary:

> When the party got to No. 4 Fort they smashed up a search light and several wires connecting mines but did not blow up the guns. On the way back they were cut off by some Turks in a cemetery. We had some difficulty in finding the point of aim, owing to the wrong bearing being passed up. The captain got furious and came and trained the gun himself. He cursed me and told me I ought to have turned Mr C___ out. It was rather a difficult position. The

Turks were driven off and our Marines got back to their boats. I did not expect half of them to come back. Only one was killed and three wounded. The one killed I am afraid was mutilated – the Turks venting their whole wrath on him. His head was smashed in, four bullet holes in his face, one in his wrist, one in shoulder and one in the knee – this was an explosive bullet and had blown his knee cap off. Both his legs were broken and a bayonet wound in his abdomen. One Marine was wounded in the eye and subsequently had it taken out, one in the shoulder and one in the chin.[7]

The Midshipman records the naval burial of the mutilated Marine, Sergeant Turnbull, on 27 February. The same day a further landing for demolition was carried out by a party from the *Irresistible* and despite stronger opposition six howitzers were destroyed. On 1 March another successful operation was carried out from the *Irresistible* on the Kum Kale Fort 4 to continue work carried out by the *Vengeance* party on 26 February, and this assisted the bombardment already begun of the Turkish defences in the Straits, which was essential if British and French minesweepers were to clear a passage through the minefields.

The attempted demolition of shore defences continued, but on 4 March this process had met with a considerable check. On this day, Marines were landed from HMS *Scorpion* and HMS *Wolverine* at Kum Kale, from HMS *Lord Nelson* to destroy Fort 4, from the *Irresistible* to destroy the bridge over the Mendere, and from the *Inflexible* and *Ocean* on the northern shore. The party from *Lord Nelson* were from the Royal Marine Brigade, and they suffered several killed and wounded, one of whom died in the boat on the way back to the ship. Some of the party were reported as missing, but later were found to be safe aboard the *Irresistible*. Sergeant William Meatyard's diary for 3 and 4 March 1915 records the landing of his battalion from the destroyer HMS *Scorpion*, in boats towed by steam pinnaces:

> Enemy shells began to fall around the boats, and there were also casualties from well- directed rifle fire. Had the enemy had machine guns I don't think many would have landed. A rifle bullet killed Sergeant Minns before we got ashore, the bullet having first passed

through and wounding Private Liversage who was sitting on his lap. We got alongside a wooden landing stage that was about 40 yards long, and clambered up on to it. Being flat without rails and being clear of obstacles it afforded no cover. We were subjected now to a good deal of rifle fire. On reaching the top we laid down flat until the first boat load had assembled. We were then given the order to stand by, and all rising together doubled to the shore. There were two who could not obey this order. We were now at the foot of the Fort, and at the commencement of the road that led directly into the village. This road I had been detailed to follow with the advanced patrol which consisted often men under Captain Brown. The advance of this patrol was not successful, we had only gone a few yards when we were compelled to lay prone and look for targets to return the fire. Out of ten, only three of us remained who were not either killed or wounded. The enemy was well concealed and apparently firing from houses. It was when on aiming (having spotted one of the enemy coming up to fire from behind a garden wall), that I got hit by two bullets from the flank, one in the chest and the other in my left foot. I wriggled back around the corner of the Fort and got my wounds dressed. Fortunately the wounds were not serious and after a breather did not feel much the worse, although lamed. No headway was made up the village road and machine guns were posted at the corner to command it whilst headway was made by another party around the other side of the Fort. The idea was to keep the enemy at bay whilst a demolition party went inside the fort and completed the destruction that the warships had commenced. A section was told off to man the crest of a bank overlooking the fort, and now I joined up with this party, being anxious to get my own back at the enemy, but they still kept well concealed.

Meanwhile the party on the right of the fort had made good progress, in fact being too eager I think they went too far, the same thing having caused disaster to the party concerned many times during the war. Overstepping the objective. They must have advanced about a mile up Yennisher Heights and were outside the Fort of that name. The Turks received reinforcements and overwhelming our small party compelled it to retire. During this fighting another company had been landed to reinforce us. A signal was sent to the senior ship, asking that the destroyers might close in and open up covering fire to assist our men's retirement. This the destroyers did with a vengeance, being able to get fairly close in, and it was as well for us that they did, otherwise I don't think many would have got back. Steaming single line ahead their broadsides of small guns simply smothered the Turks, who were prevented from following up their successful counter attack. The necessary destruction inside the fort having been carried out we re-embarked at 7 p.m., the wounded going off first, and we were put on board HMS *Irresistible*. Our losses were 19 killed 36 wounded and 5 missing. I think the enemy must have lost heavily especially from the destroyers' fire, as it surprised them. Volunteer crews were soon available from the sailors and marines belonging to the Ship's Company, and they proceeded to pull boats to shore and searching for the missing wounded or otherwise, and so well did they carry out their work, that there were only five missing as already stated. From the Irresistible I was transferred to the Hospital Ship S.S. *Soudan*, and from there to HMS *Inflexible*.[8]

By mid March, it had become clear that the plan to sweep the minefields had failed. In response, Admiral John de Robeck, the Royal Naval commander in the Dardanelles campaign, proposed to launch a major daylight attack on the fortresses, suppress them as best as possible at longer range, and to clear the minefields at the same time. This would then allow the battleships to demolish the forts at close range. Ottoman opposition was expected to be heavy, as they had been reinforcing their defences throughout the campaign; by this time, they had massed forty-two guns of eight inch diameter or larger, along with numerous mobile field guns. The attack was launched on 18 March, and *Irresistible* was again part of Second Division, which formed the second wave of the attack. *Irresistible* joined the fray at 14:39 hours, shortly after the French battleship *Bouvet* was mined and sunk in the straits; she and several other battleships then attempted to suppress Ottoman guns that were firing on boats that were picking up survivors from *Bouvet*. *Irresistible* engaged the 'Namazieh' Battery, which at that time was not actively firing. She

HMS *Irresistible* sinking off Anzac Cove, Gallipoli. (*Public Domain*)

quickly came under heavy fire herself from the 'Hamidieh I' battery, which targeted the ship with four-shell salvos.

At 15:14 hours, *Irresistible* was rocked by an explosion, and by 15:32 hours, had begun to take on a list, prompting de Robeck to order her to withdraw to avoid further damage. At 16:25 hours, *Irresistible*, having idled her engines, struck a mine that caused extensive damage to the ship. The mine detonated under her starboard engine room, flooding it and killing all but three of the men on duty there. The bulkhead that divided the starboard from the port engine room collapsed under the sudden weight of water, disabling that engine as well. Unable to manoeuvre, with a list of 7 degrees to starboard, and down by the stern, *Irresistible* became an attractive target for the Ottoman gunners. An account of the sinking of HMS *Irresistible*, and the story of how she died fighting, was told in stirring words by Lance Corporal F. Powell, of the Royal Marines, who wrote:

> It seemed to us that the *Irresistible* was being made the sole target judging by the number of shells that fell around us, although, of course, such was not the case. One of the chaps in our crew remarked, with a grin, 'something will happen in a minute, it is getting

hot.' And, sure enough, something did happen. We had just been hit again forward by another big shell that shook us all up, and then before we had time to recover ourselves, a tremendous shock was felt. Fully half a dozen of our crew were thrown violently over, and when order had been regained there was the old Irresistible heeling over to port at an angle of fully 45 degrees, and our gun pointing in the air, for all the world like an anti-aircraft gun.

Except for the men who had been thrown down picking themselves up, nobody had moved in our casemate. All we could do was to wait orders, looking, meanwhile, into each other's white, set faces. But we were not to remain long waiting. Orders came along to clear the casemate, everybody to get on deck. So, opening the casemate doors, we trooped out, wondering what would be the next thing to happen. Suddenly a man standing right aft pointed to the entrance of the Straits, and we could see, far away, a destroyer or boat of some sort speeding towards us, smoke flying from her funnels, a welcome sight indeed. The Turks ashore must have quickly realised how helpless we were, for instantly scores and scores of guns were trained upon us, and the shells began to drop all round. Truly a most uncomfortable position for us: over 600 men, helpless, forced to stand and endure this! But the hour of our deliverance was almost at hand. Nearer and nearer came the destroyer, and finally, while hardly decreasing her speed, she came up alongside. Our captain, who all this time had never left the bridge, despite the now constant hail of shells, gave the order: 'Boys and ordinary seamen, in the boat.' Followed by the order, 'All hands next!' Our turn at last! From a dozen different places we streamed over the side into the destroyer and safety.[9]

The pre-Dreadnought battleship HMS *Prince of Wales* arrived off the Gallipoli Peninsula on 1 April 1915, as part of the naval reinforcement sent by Britain following the failure to force the Narrows on 18 March. Captain Godfrey Oppenheim had joined her in January of 1914, as senior Royal Marine officer. He wrote in his journal on 5 April of the problems inherent in the present situation, and addressed the basic issue of how the navy could achieve success, in an operation with an objective which was not maritime, but landward and political:

We have cleared the Straits for about 11 miles, but the problem of how to get through the Narrows without too great loss still confronts us … we have achieved nothing, up to date beyond breaking up a few old forts, & disabling permanently a small number of guns … Nothing can be done until the Army is landed, if they can find one to land. … If this is not so, the whole schedule has been conceived by men ignorant of war; we cannot spare an Army of our own without weakening forces in France more than we can afford to; on the other hand we cannot force the Dardanelles without strong land forces. Already we have lost several ships & expended millions of pounds of ammunition – for nothing.[10]

On 21 April, four days before the historic landings on the Gallipoli beaches, he wrote in his diary some details of the forthcoming operations. Though only a junior officer, he had a clear understanding of the strategic imperative for the action:

The object of these operations is to seize the Gallipoli Peninsula with a view to silencing the guns on the Asiatic side, & destroy the torpedo tubes, there-by securing the passage of the Dardanelles for the passage of transports & merchant ships. The fleet will then proceed, accompanied by transports, up to Constantinople. Altogether we have here at present at least 100,000 men.[11]

Optimistically, he continued with the opinion that the operation would take a week, the ships would use nets to catch floating mines, and that the Turks had expended most of their 320 millimeter artillery ammunition with no resupply available. The evening before the landings he wrote: 'It was an inspiring sight to see the huge transports steaming out, their decks crowded with cheering men; and our band of course playing appropriate airs.'[12]

The next day, HMS *Prince of Wales* was off the beaches of Anzac Cove, supporting the Australian and New Zealand landings there. Indeed, she was so close to the shore that two rifle bullets struck her quarterdeck. Several men were also struck by spent bullets. Even though these were at the end of their trajectory, they still carried enough force to cause injury, and one man had to have the bullet removed from his arm by the Paymaster, all of the ship's doctors being away with the landing force. Oppenheim now decided that discretion was the better part of valour, and went below for a game of Patience in the Wardroom.

Once the landings had been achieved, the primary function of the Royal Navy assets offshore was to provide fire support using their main armament. This was not without difficulties. Naval guns, with their high muzzle velocities, flat trajectories and often unsuitable ammunition, were hampered in their ability to provide artillery support for the troops ashore. Oppenheim was involved in this and recorded the fact that all too often the lack of aerial spotting from either balloon or aircraft affected success. Without this, in addition to mis-directed fire, other problems arose as well, such as misidentification of targets. On 28 April, *Prince of Wales* prepared to fire a requested support mission – with the target appropriately 'identified'. Oppenheim then recorded what happened: 'We were instructed to knock out a big gun which was being dragged into position by a team of horses. An aeroplane spotter was to spot for us. However the waterplane had to descend owing to engine trouble. Gun turned out to be some horses drawing a plough.'[13]

Typical was his comment on 2 May:

> This morning at 5 am firing commenced but our aeroplane broke down & had to descend. We fired without any spotting, of course not knowing what effect our shot had – probably none, although those that fell on the land may have warmed up something' … We opened fire on a column of Turks this morning with 12 pdr cannon with great success – bits of Turk could be seen flying about. The kite balloon is doing good work spotting now. Agamemnon knocked out 3 guns this morning with her assistance. The great point about it is that Woodward is a good spotter & knows exactly what information is required by ships …It was a fine sight to see the mass of shells bursting on & over the ridge; a really wonderful spectacle – I'm sorry for the Turks, if there were any there. But with our usual stupidity the proposed attack & the various squares allotted to ships was made en clair each ship having to indicate by flags the squares they had to fire on: so that Turks probably cleared out of their trenches in time. However we shall see.[14]

On 22 May, HMS *Prince of Wales* left the Dardanelles when she was transferred to the Adriatic to assist the Italian navy against the fleet of Austria-Hungary. It was perhaps fortuitous, because three days later, another naval disaster occurred. HMS *Triumph*, which had supported the landing of Australian and New Zealand troops in April, and which was continuing to cover them with fire from her heavy guns, was underway off Gaba Tepe, firing on Ottoman positions, with torpedo nets out and most watertight doors shut, when at about 12:30 hours she sighted a submarine periscope 300 to 400 yards off her starboard beam. It belonged to the U-boat U-21 under the command of Lieutenant Otto Hersing. *Triumph* opened fire on the periscope, but was almost immediately struck by a torpedo, which easily cut through her torpedo net, on her starboard side. A tremendous explosion resulted, and *Triumph* took on a list 10 degrees to starboard. Sergeant F. Edgar Goodman, RMLI (the son of Mr H. Goodman, of Hillside House, Bleadon, near Weston-super-Mare), was serving in HMS *Triumph* at the time of this incident, and was afterwards posted as 'missing.' Later he wrote to his parents announcing his safety, and giving some remarkable details of the sinking. He stated:

> Just a line to tell you I am safe on board HMS *Blenheim*. Poor old *Triumph*! She did splendid work, and I can't well describe my feelings when she went down. I was in the fore control station (situated high on the foremast), and saw the submarine come up and fire her torpedo and watched its course until it bumped. Then I thought it was time I bumped – out of it, and I did. Took off my shoes, cap, and coat, gave a hand in helping to throw out wood to those who could not swim very well; then off I dived and was pulled up by a small boat, just as the ship went down. But, bless me, the boat was peppered full of shrapnel holes, and we had to bale out just as fast and hard as we could. Just managed to keep her afloat till we got alongside a trawler. I feel quite all right now, and fit for anything. But it seems so funny having nothing at all left – letters, photos, banjo, kit, war relics, everything is gone. Never mind, however, the main thing is having myself left. The enemy would have risked anything to get the old *Triumph* after all the magnificent work she had done.[15]

The Battle of Jutland, the largest fleet to fleet action of the First World War, was fought between 31 May and 1 June 1916, when a force of German ships entered the North Sea in a bid to lure the faster and lighter-armoured British Battlecruisers away from the rest of the Grand Fleet and destroy them in detail. The action quickly became general. Just over 100 years previously, the Royal Navy had relied upon a large pool of merchant sailors upon which it could draw to man its ships. Now, in the age of the dreadnought and super dreadnought battleship, the roles carried out on board ship were becoming increasingly specialised. When centralised fire control was introduced in British warships in 1904, they acquired a fire control team of between twenty and fifty men. Their role was to receive, record and calculate range, course and speed information relating to enemy ships and to convert this data into information for the big guns. Musicians were believed to have special aptitude for this kind of role – almost as a human computer – and between 1904 and 1912 the number of Royal Marine bandsmen, who made up the bulk of these teams deep inside the heart of a ship, had tripled. Jutland would be their ultimate test in this war – a clash of arms between British gunnery skills and practices, and those of the Imperial German navy. Overall, there were 6,000 marines present at Jutland.

Major Francis John William Harvey VC, who in his dying moments flooded the magazine of HMS *Lion*, thereby saving the ship.

At about 16:00 hours, on 31 May the battlecruiser HMS *Lion* was badly hit, a shell striking 'Q' turret at the junction between two nine inch armoured plates, and putting it out of action – an eye witness said that the top of the turret and been peeled back and opened like a sardine tin. Several fatal casualties were caused and the ship would, without doubt have been lost save for the presence of mind of Major Francis John William Harvey, Royal Marine Light Infantry, who though fatally wounded (opinion differs on exactly how – some reports say he was badly burned, others that both of his legs had been blown off) realised the imminent danger and gave the necessary orders to close and flood the magazines below the turret. This action prevented the flames from the burning cordite in the turret from reaching the rest of the ammunition and causing a massive explosion. This action on his part, which gained him a posthumous Victoria Cross, saved the ship. Harvey was appointed as second lieutenant in the Portsmouth Division of the RMLI in 1892, after passing out of the Royal Military Academy Sandhurst. He then spent time at the Royal Naval College, before returning to his division. His first seagoing appointment was to HMS *Wildfire* in 1894, and he soon began to immerse himself in the theory and practice of naval gunnery, a topic which would come to dominate his career. He soon passed as a gunnery instructor and in between sea going appointments was assistant gunnery instructor at Portsmouth, and later gunnery instructor at Chatham. His thoroughness and professionalism brought him to the attention of the commander-in-chief, and when the position of senior marines officer aboard the new battlecruiser HMS *Lion* became available in 1913, the by now Major Harvey was an obvious candidate.

On the morning of 1 June 1916, in a ceremony attended by Admiral Beaty, his body and those of ninety-eight of his shipmates were committed to the deep. The melancholy aftermath of Harvey's action came a day afterwards; when the battered ship returned to Invergordon it fell to another officer, Lieutenant Sam Bassett, and his men to remove the bodies of fellow Marines who had been in the magazine when it was flooded, and who had been drowned. Harvey's VC was presented to his widow at Buckingham Palace later that year, and some time afterwards the family presented it to the Royal Marines Museum, where his medals are now displayed beneath a portrait of the man about whom Winston Churchill wrote: 'In the long, rough, glorious history of the Royal Marines there is no name and no deed which in its character and consequences ranks above this.'[16]

Shortly after 18:00 hours on 31 May, shells from SMS *Lutzow* struck HMS *Invincible*. A few seconds later there were red glows all over the ship, and at 1834 *Invincible* blew up. A shell had penetrated her midship turret and the magazines below had detonated, blowing her to pieces. Bombardier Bryan Gasson of the Royal Marine Artillery had enlisted as a boy bugler, in 1911. His service record shows that he was just 5 feet tall, but by the time he was 18 and became a gunner, two years later, he had grown 8 inches. Now he was operating as a rangefinder in the turret of *Invincible* and somehow survived. He recalled:

> Suddenly our starboard midship turret manned by the Royal Marines was struck between the two 12 inch guns and appeared to me to lift the top of the turret and another of the same salvo followed. The flashes passed down to both mid-ship magazines containing 50 tons of cordite. The explosion broke the ship in half. I owe my survival, I think, to the fact that I was in a separate compartment at the back of the turret with my head through a hole cut in the top. Some of the initial flash must have got through to my compartment as I was burnt on the hand, arms and head – luckily my eyes escaped, I must have instinctively covered them with my hands. The rangefinder and myself had only a light armour covering, I think this came off and, as the ship sunk, I floated to the surface. After about an hour the destroyer HMS *Badger* approached, lowered boats and picked the survivors up. Luckily for me the destroyer carried a doctor and my burns were carefully treated.[17]

The cruisers HMS *Glasgow* and *Cornwall* were locked in a duel with SMS *Leipzig*, which though battered was still returning fire. By ten minutes to seven, the *Leipzig* was on fire everywhere, though her flag was still flying and her guns occasionally responding. The two British cruisers then stopped firing for a little, but dared not draw near for fear of a torpedo attack. Blazing in every corner, with her sides red hot, and with great gaps in her torn by the lyddite, it seemed now that every moment must be the *Leipzig*'s last; but still she floated and would not strike her colours. Fire was again reopened, therefore, although, as one of the *Cornwall*'s officers said, 'We all hated doing it,' and, half an hour later, she sent up a couple of rockets signifying that she surrendered and asking for help.

What her condition was then like has been vividly described by Private Whittaker of the Royal Marine Light Infantry. He wrote to his mother,

> When we went right close, she looked just like a night-watchman's fire bucket, all holes and fire.[18]

The Battle of Jutland, the largest naval engagement of the First World War and the greatest clash of battleships in history, was over. The British had lost three battlecruisers, *Queen Mary*, *Indefatigable*, and *Invincible*; three old armoured cruisers, *Defence*, *Warrior*, and *Black Prince*; and eight destroyers. The Germans had lost the battlecruiser *Lutzow*, four light cruisers, five destroyers, and the old battleship *Pommern*, torpedoed by a British destroyer in the last minutes of the confused night actions of 1 June and sunk with all hands. Outnumbered by almost 30 per cent, the Germans had inflicted far greater losses on the British and quickly claimed a victory. The Royal Navy, having twice lost the chance of inflicting crippling damage on the German battle line and then trapping the High Seas Fleet in the North Sea only to let it slip by in the dark, felt thoroughly frustrated. As their ships returned to port, the dismayed dockyard mateys threw rivets at them.

Numerous British liners were requisitioned as Auxiliary Cruisers in this war, and one such was HMS *Laurentic*, a former White Star Line passenger ship. Among her Royal Navy crew was a Marine, Private Frederick A.M. Went, RMLI, the only son of Mr Fred Went, Verger at St Paul's Church, Ramsgate. The travels of the ship were well documented by the diary of this young man, who lost his life on 25 January 1917, when HMS *Laurentic* was mined in the Irish Channel and 349 officers and men were killed, not by drowning but by exposure and hypothermia in their lifeboats. He was then 20 years of age, and after his death his father received a medal for good conduct awarded to the son by the Committee of the Marine Society, the controllers of the training ship HMS *Warspite*, where Private Went received his first training.

His diary covers the voyaging of the *Laurentic* while in commission for patrol work, a great portion of which was in the Eastern seas. The early part also refers to the attack on the German ship SMS *Königsberg*, which had taken refuge in a river on the African coast. The men on board were instructed to keep a sharp look-out for the German armed liner SS *Kronprinz Wilhelm*, and the captain offered £5 to the first man who sighted her, but it was later learned that she was interned at Newport, USA. Incidents of life on board ship are noted, and Private Went records that the attack on the *Königsberg* was on 6 July 1915. HMS *Hyacinth*, *Pioneer*, *Pyramas*, *Larconia*, *Weymouth*, *Mersey*, *Severn* and *Laurentic*, with some whalers, all took part in the operations, together with two aeroplanes. The first bomb dropped from the latter set fire to the forepart of the enemy ship. Journeys to and from Rangoon are referred to in the early days of 1916, and at Manilla Bay (in the Philippine Islands), 'We took off nine prisoners, with £9,000 in English gold on them.' On 10 February the writer says: 'Ran into tail end of N.E. Monsoon and passed Formosa during the afternoon.' A day so later, patrolling off Shanghai, he records 'been away from England twelve months.' From an American mail-boat on 18 February, thirty-eight Germans were taken, their wives and children being left. The next three months passed in patrol work in the same district, the days being occupied with the usual ship's routine. On 6 June, Private Went says: 'At sea; heard heavy gun-firing. Great excitement on board. Nothing doing.' Then comes a change: 'June 28th – left Singapore. Good-bye to the East. On our way to Simon's Town.'[19] The *Laurentic* arrived there on 17 July and at Cape Town two days later, took in 2,880 tons of coal and left on 24 July for unknown destination. The veil was lifted on 15 August, when the ship reached Halifax, Nova Scotia, and ten days later was inspected by HRH the Duke of Connaught, Princess Patricia of Connaught, and Vice Admiral Patey. She left Halifax on 29 August and commenced patrol duties off Baltimore, New York and Long Island. She was subsequently ordered home. The diary does not go beyond 8 September; but in a brief letter Private Went records his safe arrival at Liverpool on 6 December, after a rather sad and troublesome voyage. He was looking forward to a period of leave. A pathetic reminder of the danger surrounding naval life in war time is the last letter received from Private Went. It occupies a place in the final pages of the diary, and, written on 17 January, states that the ship was due to leave Liverpool again in couple of days' time. She left as arranged – and never returned. The log of the dead Marine brings home vividly to the varied and arduous work carried out by the navy in all seas, away from the major set piece battles which are most vividly remembered.

Royal Marines of Wanstead Battery, Barbados c.1917. (*Author's Collection*)

It also speaks to a service quietly performed without reward, and of the courage and spirit of the men of the fleet.

In May 1917 orders were issued for a party to be detailed for a duty, which surely was as strange as any ever allotted to the Royal Marines in the First World War. Enemy submarines were now ranging further afield than ever, and possibly to conserve their torpedo supplies, were frequently surfacing for the purpose of using their deck armament to attack defenceless shore targets. Surface raiders were also known still to be at large. It was thought that such attempts might be made against the scattered West Indian islands, then part of Britain's empire. A party of ten NCOs and forty men under Lieutenant Colonel J.R.H. Homfray was ordered to sea along with a number of 4.7 inch guns and mountings. The NCOs and men were drawn equally from all RMLI divisions.

The party left Liverpool in the SS *Olympic* on 12 May 1917 taking six guns with them. Another four guns followed in a second ship but this was sunk, necessitating replacements. Upon landing at Halifax, Nova Scotia they were transferred to HMS *Drake*, making their way south to

Bermuda. Here, Colonel Homfray made a rough selection, using charts, of probable places that the guns could be mounted. The first port of call was St Kitts, followed by Antigua, Montserrat, Dominica, St Lucia, Barbados, St Vincent, Grenada and Trinidad. At each place a preliminary survey was made with the local authorities, to ensure that the locations chosen were suitable.

At Trinidad, everything was unloaded and the men and stores were accommodated in the grandstand at the racecourse. Here, the guns and crews were divided up and allocated to their respective islands. With the work in hand in Trinidad to set up two guns, Colonel Homfray set off in a yacht, HMS *Eileen* to the other islands, taking with him the base plates, bolts and plans for the guns. At Barbados, the gentlemen of the island provided invaluable help in loaning their ox teams, carts, engines and trucks to move the gear up to high ground. Each gun was manned by one NCO and four men. The parties were to be self contained and equipped with camp equipment and all necessary stores. On Grenada it was found that the road up to the gun position was too steep for oxen to cope, and so the whole populace, men, women and children turned out to haul it up to the Morne, 573 feet above sea level. The guns at Barbados were mounted to cover Bridgetown, and were ready by 17 September 1917. At Dominica, the gun and pedestal were moved into position to cover Roseau Roads by means of a raft made of two barges lashed together, then pulled up 350 feet above sea level. On St Kitts it was positioned to cover Basseterre. On St Vincent the gun was at Kingstown.

In all cases the officers were selected from gentlemen serving with local forces who were too old for or who had been medically rejected from the British West Indies Regiment. Most of them served without pay and combined the work with other duties. All Royal Marine gunners and privates were made acting bombardiers in order to give them command over the gunners who again were local men who had been rejected from the British West Indies Regiment. These NCOs spent a great deal of time drilling their men so that they became highly proficient. They very quickly gained a soldierly bearing and were even able to turn out guards for their respective governors. The detachments cultivated gardens and grew vegetables. The locations in some cases were quite lonely and in order to relieve the monotony exchanges were carried out between batteries.

Royal Marines of Wanstead Battery, Christmas 1917, Pte Clowhurst, Cpl Welch, Pte Jennings, Pte Pamplin, Pte Knott. (*Author's Collection*)

In many cases the men lived alongside the local populations and made themselves popular.

They were not called upon to fire a shot in anger, but valuable experience was gained. It is not known if the enemy were aware of their presence; if so, they might have had a deterrent effect. After the Armistice they remained in situ for three months, and then orders were received to pack everything up. The first party left Trinidad in February 1919 and picked up the rest in succession, returning via Bermuda and St Johns, New Brunswick.

Royal Marines also served aboard ships on the Atlantic convoys, after this system was introduced as a means of defeating the predatory U-boats, which had taken such a toll of British merchant shipping. It was dull and monotonous as Lieutenant Sam Bassett remembered:

In February 1918 I was appointed to HMS *Isis*, where I relieved Lieutenant Robert Sturges, now [Lieutenant General] Sir Robert Sturges. Isis was an old cruiser employed in convoy work between Glasgow and Nova Scotia. The other end of the line was actually not

Nova Scotia at all, but the United States, because convoys usually gathered in Chesapeake Bay, and Isis used to pick them up there and escort them to Nova Scotia before making the Atlantic crossing. She was a slow cruiser, but so were the convoys, and crossings normally took twenty-eight days.

There was no bakery on board, and of course no refrigeration, so three or four days from port we were forced back onto hard tack. This was an abysmally dull sort of life, even worse than Scapa – where at least I had my golf! – and only on two occasions were we ever attacked by submarines. Once they downed a transport carrying army mules, and I had to order my Marine detachment to shoot the poor beasts as they struggled in the water. On another occasion Isis rushed to Halifax on rescue work after the port had been almost destroyed when a TNT ship blew up.[20]

During the latter part of the First World War many men of the Royal Marines were also seconded to the merchant service as gunners, to try to provide some protection against German submarines on defensively armed merchantmen. One example was SS *Hunsgrove*, a British steamer of 3,063 tons. On 8 June 1918, *Hunsgrove*, on a voyage from Cardiff to France with a cargo of coal, was sunk by the German submarine U-82 (Heinrich Middendorf), 6.5 miles north-west from Trevose Head in Cornwall. The bravery of the marines in this instance came to light at a subsequent Coroner's hearing, as reported in the *Cornishman* under the headline 'Plucky Royal Marines. Splendid Story Related at Penzance':

> A splendid story of pluck and devotion to duty, and one which redounds to the honour of the men of HM Services, was revealed at an inquest held by Mr. W. Dennis Lawry at Penzance on Saturday evening. On a certain ship which was torpedoed in the very small hours of the morning, there were serving as gunners a lance-corporal and three privates of the R.M.L.I. When the torpedo struck the ship the crew took to the boats and pulled away from the vessel, but Joseph Butler, age 40, a coloured greaser, failed to get away. He, however, found that three Royal Marines were on board. They had declined to leave the ship, and were standing by the gun. When

asked why they remained when the crew had left, one replied that it was their duty to stand by the gun in the hope of engaging the enemy submarine. They found the ship was rapidly foundering, and the three of them, with Butler, jumped overboard. All got hold of wreckage. None of the ship's boats were in sight, but three or four hours afterwards they were rescued by a patrol boat. The four were a bad way, and Butler was unconscious. Artificial respiration failed to restore him and at the inquest it was stated that death was due to exhaustion and drowning. The coroner and the jury congratulated the marines on their courage and devotion to duty.[21]

More heroism in a sinking vessel was shown on 9 November 1918, just two days before the end of the war, when the pre-dreadnought battleship HMS *Britannia* was torpedoed by a U-boat off Cape Trafalgar. She was to be the last major capital ship lost in the war, and she went down with considerable loss of life. After the first explosion, the ship listed 10 degrees to port. A few minutes later, a second explosion started a fire among the 9.2 inch cartridges, which in turn caused a cordite explosion in the magazine. Darkness below decks made it virtually impossible to find the flooding valves for the magazines, and those the crew did find were poorly located and therefore hard to turn; the resulting failure to properly flood the burning magazine probably doomed the ship. *Britannia* held her ten-degree list for two and a half hours before sinking, allowing most of the crew to be taken off. Most of the men who were lost were killed by toxic smoke from burning cordite; fifty men died and eighty were injured. Among her crew was a lieutenant of the Royal Marine Light Infantry, Harry Day, who had been nicknamed 'the Boy Sprout' when he first came aboard as a teenage probationary second lieutenant, straight out of Chatham Depot, on account of his prodigious increase in height as the months went by. He was awarded the Albert Medal (Sea) second class for fighting his way through the smoke and cordite fumes twice to rescue two injured men trapped below deck. Hearing groaning and unable to reach the Wardroom through the jammed door he burst the pantry hatch and climbed through to find the two wounded. He then fetched two stokers from the Quarter Deck to help him bring the dying men through the hatch, and carry them to the forecastle. The citation for the award of the Albert Medal continues:

Marines and sailors onboard ship at Scapa Flow, 1918. (*Author's Collection*)

….During his first visit to the ward room, Lieutenant Day was alone, in the dark, the ship with a list and fire close to the 12in magazine. While carrying out this rescue work he inspected all scuttles and deadlights in the ward room (and cabins before it) and ascertained that all were properly closed before leaving. The cordite fumes were very strong, and his life was in danger throughout. His courage and resource were beyond praise.[22]

The fact that one of the men rescued was the Ward Room steward gave Day the opportunity, later, of remarking dryly that he was only trying to save the keys to the bar stockroom. He was gazetted for the Albert Medal on 7 January 1919 and received the decoration at Buckingham

A group of marines aboard HMS *Curacoa*, in 1918. They are sporting a motley collection of German souvenirs. (*Author's Collection*)

Palace from King George V on 13 February 1919 (becoming only the third Royal Marine to receive the AM). In 1971, Albert Medal holders became eligible to exchange the award for the George Cross, which Day did. He later transferred to the RAF, and as Wing Commander 'Wings' Day was one of the participants in the famous 'Great Escape' from Stalag Luft III.

Marines were renowned for their caustic sense of humour, but sometimes they were given as good as they gave. Private George Lowe from Birkenhead remembered that after the *Britannia* was torpedoed, and the order 'Abandon Ship' had been given, the crew had to make their way as best they could to a destroyer which had pulled up alongside:

> Hawsers were run from the *Britannia* to the destroyer, down which we swarmed. Some got across. Others were not so lucky. One of the unlucky ones who had a free bath was a Cockney stoker nicknamed 'Shorty,' who, after splashing and struggling about, managed to get near the destroyer.
>
> To help him a burly marine dangled a rope and wooden bucket over the side, this being the only means of rescue available. The marine, who was puffing at a large meerschaum pipe, called out: 'Here y'are, Shorty, grab 'old o' this bucket an' mind yer don't drown yerself in it.'
>
> 'Shorty' makes sure of bucket, then wipes the water from his eyes, looks up to the marine, and says: 'Garn, give the kid 'is trumpet back.'[23]

The experiences of the Royal Marines in the war at sea between 1914 and 1918 underlines how diverse their skills were, as gunners, signallers, and as boat crew and shore party men. In different climates and different oceans, the high standard of their training was evident. Many experienced the danger of shipwreck, through direct combat with the enemy, or through torpedo or mine strikes. The versatility of shipboard marines is also underlined by the fact that large numbers of them also undertook a stint of service with the Royal Marine Brigade on land.

Chapter Four

The Western Front 1916–1918

With the ending of the Gallipoli campaign, the bulk of the troops released for service elsewhere would be redeployed to other theatres of war. For most, including the Marines of the Royal Naval Division, this would mean a return to the Western Front, where some had served at the very outset of the First World War. These men however were in a minority, as the active service battalions had been reinforced again and again with fresh drafts of short service recruits, who had been enlisted for the duration of the war only. This did not however mean that the battalions which would now see action in France were any less well trained, indeed nothing could be further from the truth. Even though the war was reaching the height of its intensity, the recruit depot at Deal still prided itself on the high quality of its training, and the standard of soldier who passed through its gates after completing it. One newspaper report gives an insight into what this training entailed:

> On the Parade Ground of the Depot of the Royal Marines at Deal one may see, at intervals, a ceremony known as 'passing out.' This is performed by a squad of young recruits who after six months training as infantrymen are leaving for one of the divisions of the corps to learn naval gunnery, and those many duties which a Marine performs when he goes aboard ship … For an hour or so the squad will pass quickly from one test to another acting first in response to spoken orders, later to signalled orders, and never, for a moment lose the perfect balance of its movements. At the command 'Fix Bayonets' eighty or a hundred glittering bayonets sparkle for a moment in the sunlight and then with a simultaneous clatter are fixed on the rifles … Now excellence in drill as everyone knows is simply a matter of hard work. Hard work can be exacted from men in many ways, but the greatest of all is tradition. The depot of the Royal Marines,

Staff Band of the RMLI Depot, Deal, on a recruiting drive at Leicester around 1915. (*Author's Collection*)

which is, as it were, the nursery of the corps, is steeped in tradition, and there is not a man or boy who passes through the depot who is not touched by it. The Marines have a particular efficiency which is all their own, and which is due to the fact that they have at all times to be ready to go to sea or take the field. They are 'soldier and sailor too', not only in fancy, but in solid fact. They have to undergo a double training, first as soldier and then as sailor. The depot is concerned merely with their training as soldiers – and the tradition of the depot says, 'The Marines are the best drilled corps in either service – we'll leave your sea training to the divisions. Meanwhile, we've got six months to make a perfect soldier of you – and its up to you to see we do it.' And they do.[1]

The correspondent went on to describe in detail some of the training which he had observed at Deal, which was perhaps lacking to a certain degree in preparing the recruits for what they would encounter on the Western Front, a landscape now dominated by barbed wire and defended by machine gun positions:

> It was my good fortune recently to see a squad 'passing out' in bayonet drill, and a very thrilling and exciting performance it is. Several lines of trenches have been dug, and the enemy, represented by stuffed sacks, is entrenched in them in full force. The squad is formed up in lines of 12 men, lying down. A whistle blows; the line rises and advances towards the trenches at the double, bayoneting the sacks as they go. A small bullseye target is pinned on to each sack, and a man making a good thrust and withdrawing his bayonet correctly takes away the target on the point of his bayonet. The last line of trench is defended by a number of swinging sacks, which represent the enemy in the 'on guard' position. From the sacks protrude clothes props, and on top swinging footballs to take the place of a human head. To deal with this formidable foe it is necessary to beat the poles to one side and use the butt of the rifle upwards against the football, a very difficult feat to perform on the run … During the first two or three weeks of his training the recruit is instructed in the duties of sentries & c, he is employed on fatigue, and later has two or three weeks devoted to musketry. Then he undergoes a course of field training, and the last two weeks of the course are given up to infantry drill on parade.[2]

After leaving Deal however, the training would be completed at the First Reserve Battalion RMLI, before posting to a battalion in the field.

The men of the Royal Marine Artillery meanwhile had remained in France since first arriving there in 1914. There had been a hope that they might provide the artillery element of the Royal Naval Division but that was not to be, and instead they formed two artillery brigades for service on the Western Front; one of super-heavy howitzers and the other of light anti-aircraft pompoms. The Howitzer Brigade RMA was formed to man 15-inch guns on field mountings. These curious weapons were distinct from the heavy weapons which were operated by the Royal Garrison Artillery. They were designed at his own initiative by Rear Admiral Bacon and a number were ordered by Winston Churchill, who had been impressed by the Austrian howitzers used by the Germans in 1914. The first two of these new howitzers reached France in 1915, the next two in March and April, and by 1916 there were ten operational.

Temporary Lieutenant Franks Lubbock Robinson, Royal Marine Artillery, was awarded the Distinguished Service Cross for conspicuous gallantry and devotion to duty as an artillery observing officer in the neighbourhood of Ypres, between 30 July and 10 August 1915, the citation stating that he was: '...posted on a high building in the neighbourhood of Ypres. The building was continually shelled by the enemy with heavy guns, but he maintained his position, a most precarious and dangerous one, even when the building was in imminent danger of falling, and supplied valuable information throughout.'[3]

RMA 3258 Colour Sergeant Herbert A. Clark, Royal Marine Artillery. He spent the entire First World War on training duties in the UK. (*Author's Collection*)

Robinson was the third son of the Very Rev. J.J. Robinson MA DD, Warden of St John's College, Winnipeg, and latterly Dean of Belfast. On the paternal side he was a grandson of the late Mr John Robinson J P, a former proprietor of the Dublin Daily Express. Born in 1886, he was a master at Eton before the outbreak of war, and represented Ireland as an international at hockey, taking part in the 1908 Olympic Games. When hostilities commenced Robinson was on holiday in the Rocky Mountains. He hurried home, and was given a commission in the Royal Marine Artillery, with which he served in the defence of Antwerp. Since then, he had taken part in severe fighting in Flanders with the Heavy Howitzer Brigade. Lieutenant Robinson's brothers, David and Norman, were officers with the Canadian Contingent.

The Anti-Aircraft Brigade consisted of three batteries, with a fourth formed slightly later. Anti-aircraft organisation was at that time non-existent, very little was known about that special form of gunnery, and as far as the RMA were concerned, everything had to begin from the beginning. The gun adopted was the 2-pounder pompom, which Colonel C.A. Osmaston adapted for the purpose. He was not only the Commanding Officer, but also the technical expert, who designed and prepared all the equipments and transport and more particularly the fuses, which he greatly developed. The guns were mounted on special motor lorries, which were armoured and carried the guns, crews and ammunition; the mounting, which was of the high-angle type, admitted of all round training and the guns were fitted with special sights. There were other lorries for personnel, baggage and stores, both armoured and unarmoured; the officers had small cars or motor cycles, so that the unit was completely mobile. Each Battery was supplied with four guns. Everything was in an experimental stage, but experience was being rapidly gained and the moral effect of the guns was very great. Owing to the short range of the gun, or rather of the fuse, it was necessary to place the batteries as far forward as possible to prevent hostile aeroplanes from crossing our lines. The gun proved that it was able to develop a very high rate of fire, which was found most effective in turning aeroplanes back from their objective if they came within range. At this time, owing to the great shortage of anti-aircraft guns, the enemy planes were flying at low altitudes. The projectile was a common shell, and so lacked hitting power at such objects and was only effective if actually burst on a vital part of an aeroplane. The RMA gunners, however, being used to firing at rapidly moving objects, were able to make good shooting in spite of many mechanical difficulties with the guns due to jams and defective cartridges. It also became evident that concealment of guns and personnel was essential, as they drew the enemy fire of shrapnel and high explosive whenever they came into action.

The heavy guns of the Royal Marine Artillery had been engaged throughout the Battle of the Somme, indeed theirs were among the few British shells that were powerful enough to smash the deep German dugouts found on that front. A wireless operator attached to the brigade remembered an incident which captured the spirit of the British soldier in this terrible battle:

Imagine (if you can) the mud on the Somme at its worst. A Royal Marine Artilleryman (a very junior clerk from 'Lambeff') was struggling up the gentle slope behind Trones Wood with a petrol tin of precious water in either hand. A number of us were admiring his manly efforts from a distance when the sudden familiar shriek was heard, followed by the equally familiar bang.

We saw him thrown to the ground as the whizz-bang burst but a few feet from him, and we rushed down, certain that he had 'got his.' Imagine our surprise on being greeted by an apparition that had struggled to a sitting posture, liberally plastered with mud, and a wound in the shoulder, who hoarsely chuckled and said: 'If our typist could see me nah!'[4]

The Royal Naval Division transferred from the control of the Admiralty to the War Office in April 1916. It arrived in France in May 1916, but considerable re-organisation had now taken place. Instead of the four Marine battalions that had served at Gallipoli, in August 1915 these had been reduced by amalgamation to only two, designated at first Chatham and Deal Battalion and Portsmouth and Plymouth Battalion. They served in France as 1st and 2nd battalions Royal Marines (3rd Battalion had been left behind on Mudros in the Aegean as a garrison force). The entire division was redesignated 63rd (Royal Naval) Division in July 1916, and training and reorganisation continued at Longpré during the summer – the division surrendering its Maxim machine guns and being equipped with Lewis guns. Companies were

RMA 1112/S Gunner Thomas Deans, Royal Marine Artillery. Born in Dublin, he enlisted there in October 1915 for hostilities only. From May 1916 he served with No. 10 Howitzer Battery in France. (*Author's Collection*)

sent in turn for training with the 47th Division in the French method of trench routine. In July 1st Battalion Royal Marines went into the frontline in the Angres sector, where Private L.J. Elliott was awarded a DCM after spending four days without food in no mans land, attempting to rescue a mortally wounded officer. The formation fought its first major action in France in November as part of the final stages of the Battle of the Somme, its objective being Beaucourt-sur-Ancre. On the morning of 12 November 1st Battalion Royal Marines was in the frontline with the 2nd Battalion forming up behind. There was a thick mist that morning and very dark when the attack began. The enemy barrage fell particularly heavily on the Marine battalions, and every company commander in the 1st was killed before reaching the German line.

CH-42 (S) Pte George Hardstaff, wounded in France on 13 November 1916, he spent the last year of the war aboard HMS *Cyclops II*. (*Author's Collection*)

Sergeant George Edwin Howard Nettleton was serving with the 2nd Battalion Royal Marines and recorded in his diary:

> Attack started 5.45 am … by 6.30am 5 of my crew knocked out. By 6.45 another two are gone. With only two men and myself left take the gun. Soon after I received a bullet in left thigh. Gave orders to other two men to get the gun back to HQtrs. I then got back in a shell hole and awaited dark. Enemy 15 yards away. About noon our artillery shelled enemy with shrapnel. Expected every moment to receive a present that was intended for Fritz. Excitement & loss of blood causes me to faint or lose consciousness which was a blessing. Dusk & I awake. Feel very weak but determined to try & crawl to dressing station. Stretcher bearers cannot come out because Fritz is firing at them as well as firing at the wounded. 2 stretcher bearers killed in trying their work of rescue. Reached our trenches safely & rolled in.[5]

One of the medical officers serving with the Royal Marines in this action was a Royal Navy surgeon, J.N. MacBean-Ross. He described the medical arrangements for the care of wounded from the 2nd Battalion Royal Marines in the attack on Beaucourt in the *Journal of the Royal Naval Medical Service*:

> Battalion stretcher bearers will lie out in the open behind their respective Companies. When the companies advance they will evacuate any wounded there may be to the Aid Post at Battalion Headquarters (St James's Street). As soon as these are dealt with the Battalion Aid Post will be transferred to that evacuated by the 1st Royal Marines in our original front line.
>
> The Battalion stretcher bearers will then, under the direction of the Battalion Medical Officer, evacuate wounded from 'No Man's Land,' handing them over to the Field Ambulance bearers, who will have a relay post in the original front line. There will be numerous Field Ambulance men to assist in the clearing of 'No Man's Land.'
>
> When Battalion Headquarters move to the new position in the green line, the Aid Post will again move and take up a position near the new Battalion Headquarters; its exact position will be indicated by a small Red Cross flag. The collection of wounded will then commence.
>
> Should cases, owing to heavy shelling or other causes, be unable to be evacuated to the Field Ambulance bearers, they will be collected in dugouts which will be marked by a wooden peg bearing a red cross with the battalion distinguishing mark underneath, thus:
>
> [image of shield with Red Cross and battalion numeral]
>
> As each successive objective is gained, a suitable site near Battalion Headquarters, and marked with a Red Cross flag, will be chosen as a Temporary Aid Post.
>
> Officers are particularly reminded of the following:
>
> (a) That every man must be in possession of a serviceable field dressing. Only very small supplies can be carried by the medical personnel, hence the dressing of a man's wound will depend almost entirely on his being in possession of a field dressing.

(b) Many officers have private supplies of morphia. This should on no account be used unless there is no chance whatever of seeing a medical officer within an hour. Morphia taken by the mouth will have no analgesic effect for at least an hour. If given hypodermically it acts in a few minutes. As the risk of a poisonous dose would be great if some has already been taken by the mouth, an additional dose, hypodermically, cannot be given with any safety.

Water – no water found in German trenches must be drunk until pronounced by a medical officer to be free from poison.
J.N. McB. Ross
Temp. Surgeon RN[6]

Another eyewitness to this action was Geoffrey Sparrow, also a Royal Naval surgeon and medical officer. He recounted the extraordinary bravery of individuals under fire:

Numerous unrecorded incidents of that advance are still fresh in my mind. To see Sergeant Meatyard of the Marines unconcernedly following behind the attacking companies, unrolling his coil of telephone wire as he advanced, was an incident typical of the coolness displayed by all ranks. It was entirely due to his initiative that telephone communication with Brigade Headquarters was kept up during the attack. The mending of this wire, when it was once established, was a matter of no small difficulty, and all of us who reached the bank on the far side of the Station Road remember

PO-928 (S) Private Rola ' Marsden, 2nd Battalion Royal Marines, killed in action on 13 November 1916 at Beaucourt. He was just 21 years of age. (*Author's Collection*)

the very gallant and successful attempts made to reopen our only method of communication with the rear. Sergeant Meatyard was eventually severely wounded, and later received a very well-deserved Military Medal.[7]

Sparrow continued with a description of the way in which by sheer force of personality a commanding officer could inspire his men to continue through the most trying of conditions:

> When I reached the Station Road above which the remains of the two Marine and Anson Battalions were digging themselves in, the only officers left in those three battalions were Lieutenant-Colonels Hutchison and Cartwright of the Royal Marines, Lieutenant-Commander Ellis and Captain Gowney of the Anson, Lieutenant van Praag and myself. All the remainder were killed or wounded, but there was no time for vain regrets. Colonel Hutchison took charge of this mixed body of men, and by his coolness, bravery, and wonderful personality, kept them cheerful and hard at work improving their position during the following two days and nights.[8]

The Royal Naval Division moved back into the line around Grandcourt at the end of January 1917, in preparation for the forthcoming attack on Miraumont. Conditions on the ground were poor; the mud which had been frozen was now beginning to thaw, turning the battlefield into a quagmire. There were no organised trenches, merely lines of connected shell holes. This made it difficult for carrying parties attempting to reach the frontline, as there were few if any landmarks to use for orientation. The attack began at 05:45 hours on 17 February 1917, with a terrific artillery bombardment. By 07:15 hours 1st Battalion Royal Marines had captured its portion of the sunken lane opposite Baillescourt Farm, and had pushed out 20 yards beyond to form strongpoints. The 2nd Battalion Royal Marines had also secured the left flank. Early the following morning a heavy bombardment indicated a probable counter-attack, and under cover of mist the enemy attempted to form up in readiness. Fortunately the mist cleared sufficiently for them to be observed only 300 yards distant, and an SOS barrage broke up the attack before it had begun.

PO-1649 (S) Private Edgar Stanley Willis was a painter with the Great Western Railway at Swindon when he enlisted. He served with the 1st Battalion Royal Marines in France between March and July 1917. This is the Royal Navy and Royal Marines version of the honourable discharge scroll, which accompanied the Silver War Badge. (*Author's Collection*)

When the brigade was relieved on 19 February the 1st Battalion Royal Marines numbered only around 100 men; it had gone into the line some 500 strong, but had suffered casualties of 7 officers and 71 men killed, and around 300 wounded. The 2nd Battalion Royal Marines had lost one officer and five men killed in the same period.

The next major action for the formation was the Battle of Gavrelle in April 1917, part of the First Battle of Bullecourt, an attempt to break through the formidable German defensive system, the Hindenburg Line. The Battle of Gavrelle saw the highest number of Royal Marine casualties in a single day in the history of the corps, with 846 recorded as killed, missing or wounded. Coming out of Gavrelle village, the 2nd Battalion Royal Marines were to advance northwards along the Gavrelle-Fresnes

Road whilst on their left the 1st Battalion Royal Marines had to advance up as far as the German trenches in the Oppy Line and then continue eastwards until they met up with their fellow marines. At 04:25 hours on 28 April the two Marine battalions launched their separate attacks. The 1st Battalion were to all intents and purposes never heard of again. They had advanced headlong into a strongpoint (where the German trench system crossed the railway line) and although some of them managed to fight their way through, the flanking units never made contact with them. The only form of news was from the few wounded whom managed to get back to their own lines. The War Diary of the 2nd Battalion for this date reads:

> 4.25 am. Battalion attacked in 4 waves the enemy trenches N.E. of GAVRELLE with one platoon under 2nd Lt NEWLING detailed to take the windmill. The windmill on the left of the Bn front was reached, but as 1st Battn RMLI on our left and 2nd Divs on their left were hung up apparently by wire, & owing to a large number of machine guns, casualties were heavy. Only two officers besides Officer Commanding & Adjutant who took part in the operations came out alive. Casualties: Killed officers 1; other ranks 25; wounded other ranks 72. Missing Officers 8; other ranks 387.[9]

Lance Corporal Bertram Nichols, a short service recruit from Odd Down, near Bath, was wounded in the back, thigh and mouth in this action, and was taken prisoner at Oppy Village. He recounted afterwards that his treatment by the enemy was not abusive, and probably what a wounded German soldier might have expected:

> I did not see any infraction of the laws of war by the enemy before capture. I was taken to a field dressing station, and my wounds were dressed there. I stayed there all night. The next day we were taken by motor to a big town – I think Douai. We were put into a church there that had been turned into a hospital. I stopped there one night, and was operated on the next day to clean the wound. They gave me some sort of anaesthetic. A German doctor operated. I do not know his name. The same day I was put on a stretcher and went to

the station in a tram. I was put into a train and went to Ohrdruf. The journey took two or three days. My wound was not touched on the journey at all. I went in a Red Cross train.[10]

Another man captured the same day was Private H. Thorne, who had received a shrapnel wound in the right arm. He was sent straight to Germany, reaching Hammelburg Hospital a week later. He recalled:

The necessary attention was given to my wound, otherwise I required no other medical attention. No medicine was given by me or required by me. I was well treated by the male nurses. We had good beds. The hospital was well built. We had not sufficient food. The rations served out daily tended to become less and less as time went on. The sanitary arrangements were good and the w.c.'s were clean.[11]

On 29 April the 2nd Battalion Royal Marines managed to gain some territory, including the all important windmill. However, by the evening all of the captured ground was back in the hands of the Germans, with the exception of that held by a small garrison, who were hanging on for all they were worth at the windmill. At one point in the action an overwhelming enemy counter-attack was stemmed only by the senior officer's rapid enlistment of his HQ staff, cooks and bottle-washers among them. Among the casualties was Sergeant Fred Shaw, the son of Frederick and Emily Shaw, of the Bull's Head Inn, Winsford, Cheshire, of the 1st Battalion Royal Marines. Shaw had already seen action at Antwerp, Gallipoli and on the Somme. He had celebrated his thirty-seventh birthday on 24 April and on that day had written to his mother, the last letter he apparently ever sent; in it he said:

PO-175 (S) Pte Joseph William Nelson, wounded on 28 April 1917 with the 1st Battalion Royal Marines, by a gunshot wound to the left leg. After recovery he was posted to HMS *Malaya*. (*Author's Collection*)

I received your very appropriate and beautiful card this morning. We are at present in the trenches, having arrived here on the 22nd. My natal day was heralded by violent bombardment and 'over the top' surely the most exciting birthday morn I have ever experienced. I thought when I read your letter about the church bells ringing, what a lucky fellow I must be to have bells at home and the booming of guns here to welcome my birthday; still I would much rather hear your voice wish me 'many happy returns.' I met a Winsford fellow the other day – young Mellor, from Over. … He came across the road where I was standing and asked if name was Shaw from Over. I said, 'Yes, if you're not a policeman'! He was billeted about 20 yards from me. So we saw a good deal of each other. I left him all right when we came to the trenches, and you can tell his people he looks very well indeed. We have got Fritz on the trot around here. Probably you have read of the terrific fighting that is taking place. The country is absolutely pock-marked with shell-holes, and what were once towns and villages are now only heaps of rubbish and brick-bats. We have been in the thick of it since I returned from leave- it's all very nerve-trying, and I wish it would end, still one must not grumble so long as one is alive.[12]

He died of wounds at the 41st Casualty Clearing Station, and on 9 May 1917 Mrs Shaw received a letter from the Sister in Charge:

I am so sorry to tell you the sad news about Sgt F. Shaw. He was brought to this hospital seriously wounded in the left shoulder. Everything that could be done was done, and he had every care and attention, but all was of no avail, and he died very peacefully this morning at 8.30. It is so terribly sad for you, and I feel for you very much indeed.[13]

The Royal Naval Division was in action again during the latter stages of the Third Battle of Ypres, when conditions on the Western Front were at their worst. By this stage the Ypres battlefield was a scene of utter desolation, a wilderness of flooded shell holes and abandoned pillboxes. Private John Brough of the 2nd Battalion wrote in his diary for 26 October 1917:

Went over the top at Passchendaele Ridge. The attack commenced at dawn. The ground was very unfavourable for us as it had been raining the night before. The whole attack was a failure owing to the ground being so muddy. Nearly all our fellows got wounded or killed, including the officer in charge, Mr [illegible]. We went too far and so got surrounded by the enemy. Stayed in the shell holes till 12 noon then tried to get back but without success so got [taken prisoner][14]

It was around this time that some growing resentment among certain members of the Royal Marines, as to their status within the Royal Naval Division, found its way into the newspapers. A letter published in the *Hampshire Telegraph* in November 1917 ran as follows:

PO-382 (S) Pte John Brough 2nd Battalion Royal Marines, taken prisoner of war on 26 October 1917. (*Copyright Mr J.A. Brough*)

> The letter which has appeared in several papers, signed 'Honour to Whom Honour …' has not come before it is wanted. It is most unfair that the gallant deeds of the Royal Marines in France should be chronicled under the title of the Naval Division. The Marine Corps has every right to be proud of its connection with the Navy, but it is something in the nature of a slight that when providing a contingent to the Army on shore its services should be lost sight of in a general description of the force of which they form a numerous and important part. The writer of the letter pertinently raises the question whether the name of this force should not he now changed to the Royal Marine Division. There is much more of the Royal Marines about it than there is of the Navy. The splendid work of

the Division from the time it was landed in Belgium to take part in the defence of Antwerp, its splendid performances in the Gallipoli Peninsula, and the excellent work it has done with the Army in France have added a lustre upon this part of the Naval forces which is nowhere recognised and appreciated more highly than by the seamen. But beyond a few Royal Naval Reserve men and the members of the Royal Naval Volunteer Reserve, which contributed to the manning of the Naval Division at its inception, it has not had a great deal to do with the sea either in its composition or its business. Even if it were not considered expedient to change the title, at least the Royal Marines, who have had so much to do with its training and who formed the bulk of its members, should receive the honour due to them for the gallant deeds they have performed, and which have added fresh laurels to their glorious record.[15]

DEAL 3795 (S) Pte Harry Hague, Royal Naval Division Field Ambulance, from Nelson, Lancashire. These men, like the divisional engineers and train, were recruited through the Royal Marines. Note the Red Cross proficiency badge on his sleeve. (*Author's Collection*)

The Heavy Howitzer Battery of the Royal Marine Artillery suffered some of its heaviest casualties during the Third Battle of Ypres, when its guns were engaged in suppressing the German pillboxes and strongpoints which dominated the battlefield. Captain Arthur Page had been serving with the Royal Marine Artillery on the Western Front in 1917, until he was seconded to an army headquarters to advise on Court Martial procedures – he was a barrister by profession. He recalled the reality of heavy battery work at the time:

> I had had no leave for nearly eleven months, and our battery had been continuously in action; the never-ceasing gun fire was beginning to affect my hearing, and it had become imperative that I should rest my

ears for a time. I had been threatened with a rest hospital by the sea, but I was lucky enough to escape with the lesser banishment which was involved with attachment to HQ for a few months until I had recovered sufficiently to return to regimental duty in the line. And so, with my gear and servant, I was whirled off to the Army. What an amazing change it was! Instead of living in the mud of the Ypres salient under a sheet of corrugated iron or a tarpaulin, with a prospect of being blown to smithereens at any moment, I found that my quarters were a comfortable hut in the grounds of a luxurious chateau.[16]

Earlier in the war, five dismounted naval guns had been landed at Dunkirk to counter the threat of a battery of German heavy guns in the suburbs of Ostend. This became known as the Heavy Siege Train. The guns were

Royal Marine Artillery gunners and their officers on the Western Front, 1917. (*National Library of Scotland/Public Domain*)

housed in concrete emplacements constructed by the RMA. Later, more naval guns were sent out and these were housed in timber and canvas structures, intended to resemble the barns typically found in that vicinity. During 1917, these batteries were engaging the German heavy guns, to assist the French and Belgian artillery, as well as to assist the monitors bombarding the sea defences. In June 1917, the British having taken over the sector in preparation for the offensive, the Fourth British Army took over both the RN Siege Guns and RMA Heavy Siege Train. In June the German 15-inch gun, known as 'Leugen boom' bombarded the town of Dunkirk; this gun was their great opponent in this sector and many duels were fought between it and the 12-inch guns, but the end of the war found both sides still in action. Casualties were not heavy, but Lieutenant Thomas Ernest Hulme, who was killed by a German shell while serving in the Royal Marine Artillery at Nieuport in Flanders on 28 September 1917, was one of the more colourful characters in this unit. The son of prosperous parents, he was born at Gratton Hall, Endon in Staffordshire. Despite his public school education he never adopted the clipped tones of his peers, and was noted for the fact he retained his Staffordshire dialect. Hulme developed early interests in debate, and was known by his school debating society as 'the Whip'. His provocative, enthusiastic behaviour got him ejected on more than one occasion from the University of Cambridge, where he read mathematics but did not finish a degree. He was thrown out of Cambridge for the second time after a scandal involving a Roedean girl with whom he corresponded. On theatre visits, he would shout at the actors; once, this led to a brawl with the police, and a weekend in prison. He kept a brass knuckleduster for use in such scuffles. He returned to his studies at University College London before travelling around Canada and spending time in Brussels acquiring languages. He had several of his works of poetry published during the war. An important book that he had written on sculpture, and which he had with him in manuscript form, disappeared from his effects after he was killed, and has never turned up. A fellow Marine officer remembered Hulme very well, and later recalled that during one of the recurring bombardments, a shell came over which Hulme, apparently absorbed in some thoughts of his own, failed to hear. He kept standing up, paying no attention, when all the others in his battery had thrown themselves down flat.

Royal Marine Artillery gunners with 15-inch shells on the Western Front, 1917. (*National Library of Scotland/Public Domain*)

On 21 March 1918 the first of the German Spring Offensives opened against the BEF in the Somme sector. The British Army was driven back over the old Somme battlefields as German stormtroopers, following behind a lightening bombardment and saturating gas attack, pushed through weak points into the rear areas. The great German offensive of March 1918, which broke through the Fifth Army front, found the Royal Naval Division on the right flank of the neighbouring Third Army. Deluged with mustard gas and high explosive, it held off German attacks all day, then reluctantly pulled back on orders from above, and for five days fought a dogged rear-guard action, which ended with the Anson and the 1st and 2nd RMLI turning on the advancing Germans and throwing them out of Aveluy Wood. Thousands of men were killed or fell into German hands as a result of the offensive; one of these was Private D.L. Grant of the 2nd Battalion Royal Marines, a 19-year-old former merchant seaman. He described the events which occurred 12 kilometres north of the Albert-Bapaume Road:

On 24th March 1918, after dusk, we lined a ridge to fight a rearguard action. We got mixed up with machine gunners and men of another battalion of the same division. I got with a machine-gun team as ammunition carrier – on reaching the edge of the ridge we found ourselves cut off. There was a gap on each side of us, and we got surrounded by the enemy. The sergeant in charge of us – I don't know his name – told us to show fight. I went to get my rifle, when I was hit on the back of the head with a rifle by a German. The sergeant then said, 'It's no use boys, there are too many of them' and we surrendered. I don't know the name of the German regiment; there were about 30 of them, and only 10 of us.

I did not actually see any ill-treatment, but there were some Germans, wearing the Red Cross badge, walking about amongst the dead and wounded. There was a great number of dead lying about, mostly Germans, but you could see a little khaki now and then amongst them. These men had knives in their hands and they were covered with blood. I didn't see them robbing or ill-treating the dead or wounded.

We were taken back behind the lines, and on reaching a village called Bus I asked for a drink, and they told me to get one out of the shell-holes. There was a great number of enemy dead lying about, and there were Germans emptying what seemed to me like paraffin over them and setting them on fire.[17]

Also in the area was Private Michael Dempsey, who recalled that on 24 March 1918 Germans in front of his positions in the Neuville area waved a white flag, to induce the British to cease fire before they advanced. He continued:

The Germans broke through on our right the day I was captured and got in our rear early in the morning, and at 8am I surrendered with two officers and about eight men. The two officers were Lieutenant P.S. Watts and Captain William, both of A Company 2nd R.M.L.I. We were all marched to Cambrai (about 36 kilometres) except Private Wheeler who was left behind to carry wounded, and he joined us again at Cambrai the following day.

At Cambrai we were two days in a cage, where we had no food for 48 hours (but they had taken away the officers and two privates). At the end of 48 hours, on the morning of the 27th, we were given each a piece of bread and then we were marched about 14 kilometres to another cage and were kept there another two days. Here we had a bit of bread and some coffee each morning, and the same at night. The second day we had some sauerkraut. I should have said that when we left Cambrai we were a party of about 1000 men, and we found already about 1000 men in this new cage. On the second day all in this new cage – some 2000 – were marched to Denain.

At Denain we had better treatment. We had our particulars taken there. There were already about 1000 there making 3000 altogether. We were billeted, some in a big marquee, and some slept in buildings close by in the centre of the town. We were fairly well fed – the sanitary arrangements were not bad, and there was a doctor, and the treatment was humane on the whole. We were not subject to any fire, being about 50 kilometres behind the line (in fact we had not been kept in any cage or place under fire from the time of capture). We were four days at Denain (when we did no work), and then 1500 of us were marched to a camp near Valenciennes, about 12 kilometres, where I stayed about 14 days.

This was a new camp which we practically made, putting up the wire etc. The sanitary arrangements here were very bad, and in the first seven days there were about 10 cases of dysentery. The food was very bad – the treatment was very harsh. I have particulars in writing of one case in particular – the death of a corporal in my company. It was Lance Corporal Proll, A Company 2nd R.M.L.I. I do not know his number. He was standing by the canal and fainted and struck his head on the kerb as he fell, and then fell into the canal. He was got out but was found to be dead – I consider this was entirely caused by starvation.[18]

Also captured on the same day was Lance Corporal T.Y. McClure of the 1st Battalion Royal Marines, who related a similar experience:

We were … captured at Havrincourt on March 24th, 1918. We were taken to a cage near Cambrai, getting no food all day. There were about 1000 British prisoners in this cage. Next morning about 500 of us were marched to a village about four hours' march behind Cambrai. There were about 1500 in the cage here, the name of which I don't know, and the only hut held barely 150 men. At 7am next morning we got our first ration since we were captured – a quarter loaf of German bread and a little jam. The food was very bad – often nothing in the morning (occasionally a little black coffee); for dinner, some vegetables cooked in water and not much of it; in the evening, quarter German loaf and a little jam. The guards behaved fairly decently. There were 14 officers in this camp in a separate hut – several of the R.N.D. and a doctor of the R.M.L.I.

On 29 March he was also taken to Denain, where he also found the conditions and treatment to be acceptable. However:

On April 7th 1500 of us were marched back to Prouvy, about 40 kilometres behind Cambrai. We were billeted in a disused sugar refinery. We slept on cement floors; no blankets and no straw, and fires were not allowed. We did a couple of hours' work a day collecting wood for the cook-house. The food was the same as in the other camps, but our bread ration failed sometimes for 36 hours. Lots of men fell sick and fainted from exhaustion. There was a lot of dysentery, and the only medicine we got was nettle leaves boiled in water. One man of the R.M.L.I. died here from exhaustion. The Germans gave permission for a private of the R.A.M.C. called Hall (a parson in private life) to write and tell his people. Private Townsend, 2nd R.M.L.I., disappeared one day, and it was said he had drowned himself; he was in a terrible state of exhaustion. One man in the R.M.L.I. was bayonetted clean through the leg one night when returning from the latrines by a guard.[19]

By the end of April 1918, casualties had so far outpaced drafting capacity that the 1st and 2nd battalions had to be amalgamated as the 1st RMLI. This would be the situation for the remainder of the war. By July a great change was noticeable – the German offensives had run out of steam, and training switched from digging defences in the rear areas to preparing for open warfare once more. After the stunning victory of the Battle of Amiens, the Royal Naval Division advanced across the old Somme battlefield again, during the Battle of Albert. Private Ernest Hobbs of the 1st Battalion Royal Marines, from Bristol, remembered:

> We were lying in front of Bapaume in August 1918 awaiting reinforcements. They came from Doullens, and among them was a Cockney straight from England. He greeted our sergeant with the words, 'Wot time does the dance start?' The sergeant, an old-timer, replied, 'The dance starts right now.'
>
> So over the top we went, but had not gone far when the Cockney was bowled over by a piece from a minnenwerfer, which took half of one foot away.
>
> I was rendering first aid when the sergeant came along. He looked down and said, 'Hello, my lad, soon got tired of the dance, eh?'
>
> The little Cockney looked up and despite his pain he smiled and said, 'On wiv the dance, sergeant! I'm sitting this one aht, fer Minnie has stepped on my toe.'[20]

PLY-1392 (S) Pte Ralph Robinson. He enlisted in December 1915 and arrived in France in November 1916. After a spell with the 3rd Battalion he returned to France in May 1918, suffering a gunshot wound in September. (*Author's Collection*)

Hobbs himself had hardly been with the battalion any length of time, for his service record reveals that he had only arrived with the battalion as a reinforcement on 15 July 1918, being posted out from the 3rd Battalion Royal Marines. His tenure was also short lived however as he was invalided home a little over two months later with a bullet wound to the right shoulder – a testament to the high turnover of casualties even at this late stage in the war. Private Hubert Trotman of the Royal Marine Light Infantry had been wounded in 1917. He returned to the frontline from hospital in August 1918, and was temporarily attached to the Hood Battalion of the Royal Naval Division as a reinforcement. With them he was involved in the final advance of the war, the so called '100 Days' offensive.

There was still heavy combat as the retreating Germans fought hard, almost to the last hours of the war. A local newspaper report described the sadness of Mrs Ellen Mulloy, of 6, Neptune Street, Birkenhead, after she received official news of the death in action of her eldest son, Private Anthony Mulloy, Royal Marine Light Infantry. He was killed on 26 September 1918. A letter which Mrs Mulloy had received from a comrade of her son stated that their battalion had just crossed a canal, and Mulloy, the writer and another soldier were left with a Lewis gun, as they took up a position behind a small mound. The gun having been got into position, Mulloy had his shoulder to it ready to fire, when he was hit by a German sniper, the bullet going right through his head and causing instant death. The writer of the letter, who sent his sincere sympathy to the family, was himself wounded soon afterwards with a piece of shell. As a boy, Mulloy worked for Messrs. Gallie Brothers engineers, of Duke Street, Birkenhead and then joined the Marines, with whom, though only 24 years of age when he fell, he had served for eight years, mainly in the North Sea. Earlier that year he volunteered for service in France, and had been out there only two months. His father, James Mulloy, was himself serving in France in a Royal Marine Labour Battalion.[21]

Trotman continues the story of the final advance, and must have been not far away when Mulloy was killed:

> As we were creeping across to a copse we came to a canal with a tree lying across it to block any barges … I had to get across, so I got down into the water, turned on my back with my rifle above me and pushed with my legs till I got to the other side. I was soaking, but squeezed my way out and made my way from cover to cover with a few shots at me until I got to the copse … Not long after that incident I was out with an officer looking for our Lewis Gun crew. We never found them. They had simply disappeared. Later

the Germans shelled the wood with gas. I put my mask on, but my eyes were stinging and everything was strange, but I was OK … At dawn we moved to a piece of high ground … [and] we were looking out on green countryside and there, down in the bottom was a whole squadron of German Uhlans. They were dismounted and lounging around. We opened up on them and the place was one mass of loose horses…In the first week of November we were still advancing, still fighting hard and losing men.

Word reached his unit of the impending Armistice at 09.45 on 11 November:

We were lined up on a railway bank nearby, the same railway bank the Manchesters had lined up on in 1914. They had fought at the Battle of Mons in August that year. Some of us went down to a wood in a little valley and found the skeletons of some of the Manchesters still lying there. Lying there with their boots on, very still, no helmets, no rusty rifles or equipment, just their boots on.[22]

Trotman was to rejoin the 1st Battalion Royal Marines the following month, when he was awarded his first good conduct chevron. Captain Harold Horne of the 1st Battalion meanwhile recorded in his diary:

During the night of 10/11 [November 1918] the front line was NE of the village of Bougnies. About 6.00 we got orders that an armistice would take effect from 11.00am when hostilities would cease and all units would remain stationary on the line then reached.

The advance started at 7.00am in a NE direction from the road north of Bougnies, passing the villages of Nouvelles, Spiennes, Harmignies to Villers St Ghislain (4 miles SE of Mons).

At 11.00am the battalion was in open fields east of the village advancing in a north-easterly direction, having found no enemy in the village and being greeted by the villagers.

At 11 o'clock when we halted, an enemy rearguard who had been firing from a wood a few hundred yards in front sent up some coloured flares – a 'feu de joie' at the ending of the war.[23]

This battalion, in the advance to victory, had fought at Albert, the breaking of the Drocourt-Queant Switch, the forcing of the Canal du Nord and the Canal de l'Escaut and in the Second Battle of Cambrai. On 11 November it was, once again, in Belgian territory, four years after the withdrawal from Antwerp. Its quartermaster, Captain T.H. Burton MC, had served continuously with the Royal Naval Division since the outbreak of war, when he had become quartermaster of the Deal Battalion. After the Armistice, the colours of Chatham Division were sent out to the battalion. In their long history none had brought them greater honour, and it was remarkable how the reputation of the Marines as fighting troops was consistently maintained, despite losses so severe as to sweep away, three or four times over, the original personnel.

Chapter Five

The Zeebrugge Raid 1918

By the end of 1917 the U-boat crisis was reaching its climax. Germany had declared unrestricted submarine warfare, which risked provoking the entry of the United States into the conflict. However Germany gambled that she could knock Britain out of the war by choking off her food supplies, before the Americans could get their troops on to the battlefield in any meaningful way. The mounting losses in merchant shipping caused grave concern at the Admiralty, in which it was believed that the majority of the U-boats in the Atlantic were operating from bases on the occupied Belgian coast. In reality, the German bases of Kiel and Wilhelmshaven were more vital to the U-boat campaign, but none the less plans were drawn up by Vice Admiral Roger Keyes to try to close Ostend and Zeebrugge harbours with blockships, and thus deny their use to the enemy. These plans were bold and daring, and in many ways foreshadowed amphibious operations that would become more common in the Second World War. Whilst shore parties of Marines were to be landed to neutralise enemy defences, block ships would be sunk at critical points in the approaches to the two harbours.

Calls for volunteers had gone out to ships of the Grand Fleet and naval establishments around Britain, and such was the enthusiastic response that only about half of those who had stepped forward could be taken. The volunteers at this point knew only that the mission was a hazardous one, though more than a few could make a guess at what it would entail. The need for secrecy and surprise was the basis of the whole plan. Partly to distract attention from the all-important blockships, and partly to overcome the defences, at Zeebrugge it was decided to land a force on the seaward side of the breakwater (known as the mole), behind or to the east of the machine-gun posts, which faced westward, and which could sweep the surface of the mole. The old cruiser HMS *Vindictive*, and converted Liverpool ferry-boats *Iris* and *Daffodil* were selected to

The Zeebrugge Raid 1918

Marines scale a gangplank from HMS *Vindictive* to attack the Mole at Zeebrugge, 23 April 1918. (From the series *Thrilling Scenes From the Great War*)

carry this storming party. The *Vindictive* was to take two companies and a machine-gun section and four Lewis guns, a trench-mortar section, two 7.5-inch howitzers, one bigger howitzer of 11-inch calibre, two pompoms and two fixed Stokes mortars. All members of these units were to be marines, drawn from the Royal Marine Artillery and Royal Marine Light Infantry, each allotted to appropriate duties for which they were specially trained. The *Vindictive* was also to carry the naval landing parties, two companies of seamen, a demolition party, and an experimental party with flame projectors. The *Iris* was to carry a company of marines, two mobile Stokes mortars, and a company of seamen; the *Daffodil* was to carry a demolition party of seamen. On arrival at Zeebrugge, *Iris* would pull up at the mole alongside *Vindictive*. *Daffodil* would push against *Vindictive*'s starboard side to keep her from drifting away from the mole. The storming parties would then land, the marines sweeping westward along the mole, covering from that direction the storming and demolition parties of seamen, who would wreak havoc among the guns on the extension and any hostile craft tied up inside the breakwater. The danger was realised of re-enforcements reaching the mole by the viaduct from the shore, and outnumbering the marines. Thus two old submarines (C.I and C.3), which were filled with explosives, were to ram the viaduct, after which they would be abandoned by their crews and be blown up, thus cutting off communication between shore and mole.

A full-scale version of the mole was taped out on chalk grassland at Freedown between Deal and Dover, where the marines practised over and over – under different scenarios – the storming of the gun emplacements. However, in order to preserve secrecy, they were told that the taped out zone represented a section of the German frontline in France, which was to be attacked by the Royal Naval Division. Had something more realistic been employed, which including disembarking from boats, then some of the difficulties that would be encountered in the actual raid itself might have revealed themselves. The men were at the same time being drilled in the rudiments of what would become commando-style training, including bayonet and 'trench' fighting. Instruction was given in disarming sentries and hand-to-hand combat reinforced by boxing and wrestling and each company included trained Lewis gunners and bombers, adept at throwing Mills grenades. The adjutant general of the Royal Marines visited during training and offered those who wished to withdraw from the expedition the opportunity to do so, and even though it was generally understood that this was a suicide mission, 'Nobody accepted the offer, so in effect every man in the battalion was a volunteer'.[1] After weeks of training, the men were in prime condition and the battalion was combat-ready.

After plans to launch the operation were twice cancelled due to unsuitable weather, the date was finally settled upon to attack – 23 April 1918, St George's Day. By this time Vice Admiral Keyes, had succeeded Vice Admiral Bacon in command of the Dover Patrol; and he was therefore in personal charge of the great adventure that he had initiated and planned with such care. Every man under him was not only a volunteer fully aware of what he was about to face, but a picked man, selected and judged by as high a standard, perhaps, as the world could have provided. Flying his own flag on the destroyer HMS *Warwick*, Admiral Keyes had entrusted the *Vindictive* to Acting Captain A.F.B. Carpenter, the *Iris* and the *Daffodil* being in the hands respectively of Commander Valentine Gibbs and Lieutenant Harold Campbell. The soldiers, consisting of three companies of the Royal Marine Light Infantry and a hundred men of the Royal Marine Artillery, had been drawn from the Grand Fleet, the Chatham, Portsmouth, and Plymouth Depots, and were together titled the 4th Battalion Royal Marines; they were commanded by Lieutenant Colonel Bertram Elliot. The three block-ships that were to be sunk at Zeebrugge, the *Thetis*, *Intrepid* and *Iphigenia*, were in charge of Commander Ralph S. Sneyd, Lieutenant Stuart Bonham Carter, and Lieutenant E.W. Billyard-Leake; while the old submarine C3 that was to blow up the viaduct was commanded by Lieutenant R.D. Sandford. Private Philip Hodgson RMLI, of No. 12: Platoon, C Company, describes their departure at 14:00 hours that day:

> It was a fine spring afternoon, when we set off, *Vindictive* with *Iris* and *Daffodil* in tow to save their limited supply of fuel followed in line ahead by the old gun boats, to become block-ships, *Thetis*, *Iphigenia* and *Intrepid* sailing down outside the Goodwins to our rendezvous off Dover with the remainder of the attacking force consisting of lines of destroyers and MLs with their special smoke generators.

It was indeed a thrilling sight to see this armada of ships sailing in perfect order in an almost calm sea as the sun set and darkness fell.[2]

The Royal Marines played the leading part in the battle which was to come. Their role was to involve the bulk of the fighting while the seamen carried out the work of demolition. Of the 400 or 500 men of the 4th Battalion Royal Marines who landed from the *Vindictive*, nearly 100 were killed or died from wounds, other total casualties were over 300. Private Bill Scorey remembered:

> … How I escaped God knows, for the first shell that hit the *Vindictive*, which our Coy was on, killed dozens and set them all aflame, all the lads round me were blown to bits and I was flung between her funnels, my tin hat was shattered and so was my rifle, but I soon found some more. We then had the order, 'Steady Pompey Company'. We were just going alongside the Mole, our section was the first to land, what there was left of us, and we were very lucky too, for no sooner were we on top of the wall, than the German machine gunners had the range, and were playing hell with us, then the heavy guns fired point blank into us, but we still advanced and soon silenced them.[3]

An unnamed Marine gave an interview after the battle:

> I volunteered for this particular job because I lost two brothers at the front in six months, and wanted get my own back. Moreover, I had a presentiment that I should come back all right, but I don't want to go through that lot again. It was hell while it lasted. I was with those who were told off to attack Zeebrugge. We arrived off the harbour all right, and had every reason to believe that we caught the enemy napping. As we steamed into the harbour the place was suddenly lit with star shells. Then the fun started. Ahead of us we saw a large German destroyer, evidently in the act of getting under way. We rushed at her at full speed and rammed her, and cut her clean in half. She sank, and we passed over her. We then steered alongside the Mole, and silently as we could we 'out gangways' and got to the Mole. It was then raining hard, and as our storming

party was forming up a big burly German loomed out the semi-darkness and made a dive for the nearest men, but before he could do anything our captain, who was calmly walking up and down, knocked him on the head with his truncheon, with which some of us had been provided. He killed the man outright. On the other side of the Mole lay another German destroyer. This vessel we destroyed, and knocked-on the head all the men who opposed us. We then received the order to charge, and rushed along the Mole to the shore. We bayoneted and shot all the men we came across. The noise of the firing mingled with the shouts and cries of the men was terrible. It was fair slaughter, and all around us was a hubbub, but we kept our heads and put the wind up the Boche completely. He was fairly caught this time. Out in the harbour we could hear and see the fighting, and when got back on board I heard that some of our attacking parties actually boarded some of the German destroyers in the harbour, the crews of which were completely taken by surprise. The coverings of their best guns had not been taken off, and as the Germans scrambled up the hatchway from below, many them only partially dressed and half-awake, were knocked on the head and tumbled back again. On shore we destroyed and dismantled all the guns we came across. We were on shore just over an hour, and what hour! When we got on board and steamed out of the harbour we crossed over the destroyer which we had cut down on entering, but fortunately for us our propellers scraped clear.[4]

Stories of derring-do in the action on the mole continued to appear in the press for several days afterwards. One marine belonging to the storming party said:

A hefty German fired at me point blank at five yards range. A bullet entered the fleshy part of my arm near the muscle. It came through my sleeve, then through my left breast pocket, and out by the button, without seriously injuring me, but my mate fixed him properly. Quickly reversing his rifle he gripped the muzzle and brought the butt end square on the German's napper, flopping him out fair. In joke I cried, 'Right-o, matey. That's the stuff to give 'em.' Another reported: I was told off to supply ammunition for our ship's gun, which lay alongside the Mole. I had got a step on deck when an enemy shell burst quite close, upsetting the lot. Fortunately for me I was knocked down, but otherwise escaped. Yet more marvellous still, not one of the shells on deck exploded. His comrade added: I belong to what you might call 'the pirate crew' that boarded one of the German destroyers. The first Hun we saw was the marine on sentry on the deck. We quickly downed him, and then made a dash for the hatchway, knocking the German sailors back much quicker than they could scramble up. Before we left I approached our old friend the sentry, and do not know whether he was dead or not, but said, 'Sorry old chap, but I am a marine myself, so there's no harm in taking your helmet.' Whilst a fourth marine said: 'A German bullet struck the rim of my steel helmet. It actually passed under the rim, then across the top of my head, and out from the other side of the helmet, making a clean round hole. All it did to me was to singe my hair.'[5]

Private Bill Scorey continued:

We then had the order to retire, but the devils started to come on the wall at us, but few got away. One fired point blank with his revolver at one of our lads, but he paid dearly for it, for our Captain (Bamford) crowned him with his loaded stick [...] We then had to come aboard owing to the tide, but had to climb up the wall again by ladders, which was about 15 to 20 feet high so it was no easy job. No sooner were we on the top than a shrapnel shell came and scattered us, some got blown back on the Mole and some in the water. I went in the water myself, but managed to get on board by a rope, which was flung to me, she then pushed off leaving some men behind. I think I was the last man aboard.[6]

Not until the mole had been cleared of every man that could possibly be removed did the *Vindictive* break away, turning in a half-circle and belching flames from every pore of her broken funnels. That was perhaps her worst moment, for now she was exposed to every angry and awakened

HMS *Vindictive*, seen after the Zeebrugge Raid in April 1918. (*Library of Congress*)

battery; her lower decks were already a shambles; and many of her navigating staff were killed or helpless. But her luck held; the enemy's shells fell short; and soon she was comparatively safe in the undispersed smoke-trails. She had indeed earned Admiral Keyes' signal, 'Well done, *Vindictive*', but as the shattered vessel withdrew under cover of smoke, Private James Feeney RMLI recorded that, on going below: 'We saw the result of our landing; one thing was certain – it cost a great deal of blood. I shall never forget the sight … dead and dying lying on the decks where, but a few hours before, they ate, drank and played cards. In the light of day it was a shambles.'[7]

The *Iris* never actually managed to land her assault party. Before she had succeeded in coming alongside, the recall was sounded. That however is not to say that she sustained no casualties. One Marine, Lance Corporal George Calverley remembered as she pulled away:

Major Eagles shouted 'All Marines below', to leave the deck clear for the sailors to work the ship. Being a ferry boat, there was a wide staircase to the deck below, which we descended, and standing with my back to the ship's side I said to one of my section about three feet away, 'Well Cornforth, the worst is over, now it's a matter of getting home – where are the others?' As he opened his mouth to answer, he gave a gasp and fell at my feet. At the same time something came through the ship's side near my left shoulder. I bent down to him and woke up five yards from where we had been standing.

We were moving very slowly, and on looking back I couldn't see the Mole or Vindictive, or Daffodil. We did our best for the wounded, which was very little because of the darkness and the severity of wounds caused by shrapnel. We were entirely on our own, and partly disabled. There appeared to be no officers around except the Naval Lieutenant who was navigating the ship. It was decided to get the ship into as good a defensive position as possible, and out of the eight Lewis Guns we found two which were serviceable, and rigged up a machine-gun on each side of the bridge. While

Detail of the superstructure of HMS *Vindictive* after the Zeebrugge Raid, showing the damage inflicted by German fire. (*Library of Congress*)

we were doing this we found the body of Commander Gibbs with both his legs shot away.

Dawn came slowly, and we were able to search around for bodies on the deck. We had obviously been hit by two heavy shells as we left Vindictive. Out of the six Marine officers, Major Eagles and numbers 1 and 2 Platoon Commanders were dead, the Second-in-Command and my platoon commander were wounded and out of action, as was number 4 platoon commander who was shell-shocked. Wounded were dying every minute in spite of the little we could do for them. I came across Gunner White [RMA] and his mortar crew, all of whom were dead.[8]

Sergeant Harry Wright, of the Royal Marine Light Infantry, had taken a most gallant part in the raid, leading one of the storming platoons. He was not on any of the ships that returned towards home. He and eleven other Marines were still on the mole. They watched the ships go with concern, but not alarm – yet. They understood that coastal motor boats would be hanging about for some time yet, to pick up stragglers. No boats came, only at 03:00 hours a German officer and fifty soldiers. The helpless marines, lost through one of the sad accidents of war, passed into captivity.

Following the Zeebrugge Raid, eight Victoria Crosses were allotted to those participating, of whom there was scarcely one that had not doubly earned the honour; four were awarded directly, to Lieutenant Commander Bradford, Lieutenant Commander Arthur Harrison, lieutenants Percy Dean and R.D. Sandford of the Royal Navy. Two recipients each from the Royal Navy and Royal Marines were also to receive the Victoria Cross, the names being selected by ballot of those involved, in accordance with Clause 13 of the original VC Warrant. For the Navy, Acting Captain (soon to be confirmed as Captain) A.F.B. Carpenter and Able Seaman Albert McKenzie were thus chosen.

The two marines selected were Captain Edward Bamford RMLI who was first on the mole and last off, and who led his men forward from position to position without regard for personal safety, and Sergeant Norman Augustus Finch RMA, of the *Vindictive*'s fighting-top. It became a matter for comment in the citation that a member of the Royal Marine

Artillery should have been selected by a unit for which the majority originated in the Royal Marine Light Infantry. The ballot was held on 26 April 1918 at the Royal Marine Depot at Deal. The men were assembled on the parade ground, where slips of voting paper were handed to those present. (It is not known whether the hospital wounded voted or not, but it is known that they were included in the list of candidates.) The original record of the Marines ballot was exhibited in 1956 at the Victoria Cross Centenary Exhibition, held at Marlborough House. It consists of a scrap of flimsy yellow paper, with all of the names under consideration written in blue crayon, with lines of ticks recording the numbers of votes received. About a score of names were listed, but the preponderance of ticks against the two chosen appears overwhelming. Sergeant Finch was later heard, in a radio interview discussing his award, to state that: 'This isn't really mine; I'm only selected to wear it on behalf of the regiment, and when I die it will have to be returned to the regiment.'9

PO-159 (S) Pte Charles Marriott. He served at Gallipoli, being wounded by a bullet in the left side of the chest on 1 May 1915. The bullet remained lodged in his lung, but Marriott went on to serve at Zeebrugge, where he was wounded again by a bursting enemy shell. He later took part in the VC ballot. (*Author's Collection*)

In fact there is nothing in the warrant to state that the medal of someone selected by ballot is any less the personal property of that individual, than one awarded for an individual act, but Finch may well have been expressing his own personal belief that he wore it on behalf of his comrades.

Although Keyes would never admit it, the blocking of Zeebrugge was not fully effective, and the two attempts to block the canal at Ostend were complete failures. But the Zeebrugge operation gave a great lift to national morale, when the country was still reeling from the news of the German March offensive in France, and went a long way to restoring the reputation of the navy, which since the inconclusive and disappointing Jutland battle had appeared inactive, indeed ineffective. The naval historian

Arthur Marder wrote of it: 'No incident in the war on land or sea had more deeply touched the popular imagination in Britain. It restored faith in the Navy.'[10]

His Majesty King George V had visited the depot at Deal on 7 March to inspect recruits under training, and whilst there had taken the salute of the 4th Battalion as it marched past. He had directed that the senior recruit squad should in future be styled the King's Squad and the best recruit in it to be awarded the King's Badge. On 28 April his private secretary wrote to the commandant:

> It is a matter of special interest to the King to remember that the 4th battalion was at Deal on the occasion of His Majesties' inspection on March 7 ... I am to assure you of the King's deep sympathy with the relatives of those who lost their lives, as well as His Majesties' solicitude for the progress of those who have been wounded, one and all having so valiantly maintained the splendid traditions of the Royal Marines.[11]

The St George's Day battle will live for ever in Britain's naval heritage, exceeding in fine seamanship, disciplined gallantry, headlong fury, and fervent patriotism almost anything that modern military history has recorded, and the Royal Marines will long be honoured as among the most glorious of its heroes. The action at Zeebrugge has been hailed by some as the 'first Commando raid', and held up as the precursor to operations such as St Nazaire and Dieppe in the Second World War. The brunt of the casualties was borne by the 4th Battalion Royal Marines, and thenceforth, as a mark of respect to those who had fallen the number was 'retired' by the corps. No other 4th battalion was ever raised again.

Chapter Six

Russia 1918–1919

As Russia gradually collapsed following the two revolutions which took place there in 1917, the worsening fighting between rival factions, and the desire to protect British interests as far as possible, meant that the British Army became involved in a new war before the last had even ended. In both the north and the south of the country, British forces became embroiled in the worsening Russian Civil War, between the 'White' forces loyal to the deposed tsar, and the fledgeling Red Army of the Bolshevik revolutionaries. Royal Marines were in the thick of the action, though it was to prove one of the most controversial episodes in the history of the corps.

The position at Archangel, where there were large stocks of munitions, was serious, for it had become Bolshevik in 1917, but on 31 July 1918, an urgent telegram was received from the White forces there, stating that the counter-revolution was about to commence, and asking for Allied support. Two hundred French troops and ninety-six Royal Marines under lieutenants Merchant and Harries, RMLI of Colonel Paterson's Force were embarked to assist, and they cleared Modyuski Island by nightfall. The Bolsheviks had departed, and when the troops disembarked at Archangel itself the following day, the loudest cheers from the local populace were for the khaki-clad Royal Marines.

The withdrawal of Russia from combat in the First World War, following the revolutions of 1917 also meant that the Allied base at Murmansk was now under threat of attack by German forces through Finland. The old battleship HMS *Glory* spent the winter of 1917–1918 there, with an enlarged Royal Marine detachment, to counter the threat. In March 1918 she was joined by HMS *Cochrane* and seamen and Marines from both ships fought against pro-German Finnish patrols near the Norwegian border.

As Germany in turn was defeated, however, a renewed danger now came from the Red Army which threatened to recapture Archangel and advance on Murmansk. A small number of Marines remained in Archangel as part of a larger Allied contingent, and in July 1918 the Royal Marine Field Force consisting of a field battery from the RMA and a machine-gun section from the RMLI reached Murmansk from the UK. A more God-forsaken place was difficult to imagine. An RAF corporal later remembered how one of these men succinctly summed it up:

> We landed in North Russia in June 1918. We were piloted in on the City of Marseilles to a jetty. We did not know the name of the place. On the jetty we saw from the boat a British marine on sentry duty. We shouted down to him, 'Where are we, mate?' He answered 'Murmansk'.
> We asked, 'What sort of place,' and he shouted, 'Lumme, you've come to a blighted 'ole 'ere. They 'ave one picture palace and the price of admission is a bar of soap.'[1]

The marines in this force possessed both lightweight summer clothing and arctic equipment for winter conditions, and were deployed along the 300 miles of railway south from Murmansk to Kem on the White Sea. In the course of the winter the RMLI trained in ski tactics and became adept as a mobile ski column. In the spring of 1919 they saw some action against Red forces, including an action in May at which a mixed Royal

Men of the Royal Marines on the march in North Russia, 1919. Note the white Polar Star formation patch worn at the top of the sleeve. (*Author's Collection*)

Marines company attacked Red troops at Urozero, and later attacked an armoured train and captured Maselskaya, before being withdrawn from Russia in July.

Between April and June 1919, a Royal Marine detachment landed by the cruisers *Kent* and *Suffolk*, under the command of Captain Tom Jameson, fought against the Red Armies on the Kama river, with a 6-inch gun and four 12-pounders and a series of small gunboats. Deep in the heart of Siberia, their only link with the outside world was the Trans-Siberian Railway to Vladivostok. Meanwhile another party under Captain Bath fought on the Volga front.

The Royal Marine Field Force was soon to be replaced at Murmansk by the 6th Battalion Royal Marines. Its task was to subdue Bolshevik forces sufficiently to allow White Russian elements to gain the upper hand, and thus allow the British to wash their hands of North Russia. The last surviving officer of the 6th Battalion Royal Marines was Brigadier Roy Smith-Hill who died in 1996, aged 99. He remembered that the battalion was formed in the summer of 1919, ostensibly to police a plebiscite held in Schleswig-Holstein, over whether the region should be in Germany or Denmark. Their duties were expected to include manning polling stations and keeping order, but mainly it was to be ceremonial work, so there was much polishing of brasses in expectation of parades. Instead, it was sent at short notice aboard the troopship *Czar* to Murmansk to reinforce Allied forces supporting the White Russian troops against the Bolsheviks. It included men who had already served for some time in France and who were disgruntled by the fact that men with less service were being demobilised ahead of them, and young recruits who had expected to be sent home after the plebiscite, as well as a number of recently released PoWs who had come straight from Germany without being given leave.

The battalion knew little about why they had been sent to Russian territory, and British government policy was weak and indecisive. The troops on the ground were never sure if they were actually at war or not. Eventually it was decided that the 6th Battalion would be sent to help hold the front in the Lake Onega region, some 500 miles to the south, until White Russian troops had been trained to hold the front themselves. However, from the moment the battalion disembarked from the train from Murmansk, things started to go wrong. At Kandalaksha they were billeted at a location known as Sussex Village, after the Royal Sussex Regiment, which had first occupied the place. The initial plan was to hold a line of outposts facing the Finnish border, but rumours began to circulate of an advance on the Russian capital Petrograd. At this stage morale was still high, and the general belief was that one British soldier was worth about ten Bolsheviks. In their first engagement, under Major A.W. Ridings RMA at Ussuna on 24 June, one company fired upon another in an unfortunate friendly fire incident. Two other companies were ambushed by the Bolsheviks and roughly handled. An attack on a Bolshevik-held village was repulsed with losses.

They were sent on to Lake Onega on 28 August where a camp was established. The following day the Portsmouth Company made an unsuccessful attack against Bolshevik positions. Red Finns, armed with machine guns and firing from well prepared positions had inflicted a number of casualties including the battalion commander, Lieutenant-Colonel A. de W. Kitkat, who had been wounded and evacuated. The advance continued through heavily wooded country, following the railway line. Patrols extended for about 50 yards into the forest either side of the track, checking for possible ambushes. On 7 September the Marines were relieved by Serbian troops, but Smith-Hill's men were to lead the attack the next day. He was given a Verey pistol and various coloured flares to indicate to the supporting Howitzer battery that it should lift its range, increase rate of fire etc.

The next morning at 08:00 hours the attack on Koikori began. Taken to a high vantage point by the battalion's Russian guide, Smith-Hill could see the church in the village, surrounded by trenches and breastworks. An advance through heavy undergrowth began towards the hamlet, but the Bolsheviks began to return a heavy fire with rifles and machine guns. When the Marines were fired upon from behind, it was at first thought to be friendly fire from a nearby hill, but it quickly became apparent that this high ground was also in Bolshevik hands. By now the Russian guide had disappeared. Smith-Hill and two men worked their way forward in order to bomb the enemy trenches, but one of these, Private Thomas Pyle from Ferryside, Carmarthen was wounded, and two other men were killed in trying to rescue him. Having been wounded in the left leg, some Bolsheviks shot him deliberately in the right leg and body and were about to leave him for dead, but others who were more humane took him prisoner, and gave him rudimentary medical treatment. However, the severity of the wound in the left leg resulted in amputation. After he was taken prisoner of war by the Bolsheviks he was to be held captive for a period of nine months. Upon his eventual return home, he was awarded the DCM for his fortitude and patriotism whilst a prisoner. The citation read: 'For Gallant Service in North Russia, where he effectively bombed hostile sangars which were holding up the advance. Subsequently as a prisoner of war he showed much determination under very trying conditions.'[2]

He gave an account of his experiences to a newspaper correspondent after he returned to Chatham:

> For nine months he was moved from hospital to prison and prison to hospital in different parts of Russia. He describes his treatment as very rough. The hospitals lacked proper appliances. A two days' ration, he said, consisted of mouldy black bread weighing about half a pound. Water was insufficient. Russia, he declared, was in a state of chaos, and he described the Bolshevik leaders as, 'more like children than anything else.' They had no idea of government, and were unable to control the rank and file.
>
> He reached the frontier in company with refugees, and for a considerable period was in quarantine. He reached home last week. Originally he was a fine, muscular man, who went in for boxing and other athletic pursuits. He is now a weak and helpless cripple.[3]

It might be added that Pyle had already seen service in the First World War and had been wounded in action with the 1st Battalion Royal Marines in 1917.

Major A.C. Barnby the senior officer was wounded in the attack, and seeing the difficulties they were in ordered Smith-Hill to pull his men back from the village and into the woods from which they had come. Command of C Company had now devolved upon Smith-Hill, as the senior unwounded officer. It was widely believed that the Russian guide who had led them into the attack had betrayed them and instead led them into an ambush. Smith-Hill left his company holding position in the wood, whilst he went back for further orders. When he returned, he found the company gathered in the Koi-Svy road, looking dejected. They claimed that a major of the Machine Gun Corps had ordered them out of their positions; when Smith-Hill confronted the major about the way he had spoken to him men, the major retorted that they did not want to fight and were no use.

The next morning, Major R.W. Laing of the Marines addressed B and C companies and asked for volunteers to return to the outpost line. Only a handful did so, the rest refused. With Smith-Hill away at headquarters, some fifty-six of his men decided on their own initiative now to return to the town of Svyatnavolok in

CH22549 Private Tom Pyle, 6th Battalion. He was awarded the DCM in North Russia. (*Private Collection*)

the rear. He was sent after them, and when he caught up with them, they seemed quite friendly and pleased to see him. When he ordered them to muster next morning, they fell in smartly, but he informed them that for leaving the frontline as they had done, they could be court martialled and possibly shot. Whether they were just young and naïve is not clear, but they did not appear to believe that they had done anything wrong. On 11 September the remainders of the companies returned to Svyatnavolok and the men rejoined their units; the battalion then returned to the rear. Smith-Hill remembered:

> A few days after our arrival in Murmansk, all the battalion officers were summoned to force headquarters and were addressed by, I think, General Rawlinson. He told us what he thought of us, saying that there were no bad men, only bad officers and that the Commanding Officer had the main responsibility. Ninety-three men were court martialled. Lieutenant Colonel Kitkat, who had recovered from

his wound, told us that as Commanding Officer he accepted the main responsibility. A few days later the battalion was drawn up in a hollow square, with the men who had been court martialled. The Commanding Officer read out the charge against them – and the punishment. Thirteen had been sentenced to death. I watched the faces of the men and saw that they merely looked bashful, not shocked. The 53 men of my company were among those sentenced.[4]

In total ninety men were tried and found guilty of mutiny by the court martial. As well as the thirteen men who were sentenced to death, others received up to five years imprisonment. Following the wounding of Major A.C. Barnby, on 8 September 1919, command of B Company, 6th Battalion Royal Marines had devolved upon Captain Reginald Hanhart Watts. Watts, appearing to suffer a mental and physical collapse, ordered his men to retire from their position. He was later found, half carried, half pushed by his men, dazed and incoherent, stating that all was lost. Unsurprisingly this rattled many of the men and caused many to withdraw without orders. He was also tried by court martial, whilst the battalion was still in Russia. In the subsequent proceedings, Captain Watts had asked Smith-Hill to act as 'prisoner's friend' (i.e. defence counsel). This he did, and in spite of the fact that the battalion medical officer Surgeon Commander Wilkinson had testified that Watts had been previously wounded at Gallipoli, and had suffered a head injury following a recent bicycle accident, he was acquitted on a charge of 'cowardice' but convicted on a charge of 'using words calculated to create alarm and despondency'. He was ordered to be dismissed from the service but in the event was 'permitted to resign his commission at his own request' on 7 February 1920.[5]

After he was cashiered, with some difficulty a suit of civilian clothes was found for him, and he returned home in a collier. Several months later he returned to Chatham Barracks and told some of the officers that he had previously served with that he was now a member of the Black and Tans and was a member of a 'murder squad' targeting IRA leaders during the Anglo-Irish War.

Shortly afterwards the 6th Battalion returned home to Chatham, but no news had yet reached the depot of the ignominious events that had unfolded in north Russia. As Smith-Hill recounted what had happened, the commandant was utterly aghast. The battalion was quickly broken up and its members posted to various ships, for fear that if they were left as a unit they might well mutiny again. However, one of those who had avoided the Field General Court Martial in Murmansk through having been in a hospital ship at the time was later tried by a District Court Martial at Chatham, and was acquitted. This cast doubt on the verdicts handed down by the previous proceedings, and on 22 December 1919 the Conservative MP Lieutenant Kenworthy asked a question in Parliament about what had occurred. The *Daily Herald* also took up the cases of the imprisoned men, and published letters from some of them. One wrote:

> I am one of the 53 men who have been sentenced to two years' hard labour on a charge of deserting His Majesty's forces in the field. We did not. After being in action for 16 hours without any food, we were told by Major Stroover RFA who was in command of operations to get to hell out of it, as we were no good, and could go where we liked, as we shouldn't have any food or clothing. So we marched to our base and received food. So they court martialled us about three weeks after at Murmansk.[6]

Another marine, described as a 'young soldier' wrote:

> Four of our platoons tried to take this village. We had about 30 casualties in our own two platoons. It would have taken three full strength battalions to take the place, and the 'Bolo' beat the British Tommy in the bush every time, because he was born to it. After we had been fighting for 14 or 15 hours with nothing to eat, the major commanding operations told us we were absolutely useless, that we were running about like rabbits, and to go to hell out of it. So we went, and for going back he put about 100 of us under arrest. Forty marines got five years' penal servitude, and we got two years' hard labour and we are discharged from the service. Justice they call it. God what a mockery.[7]

The Admiralty began to row back from its previous position, particularly in view of the fact that eight of those convicted were under 19 years old, and none of the death sentences were actually carried out. The ninety mutineers had been shipped to Bodmin prison, where they continued their resistance to arbitrary authority. This resistance paid off. The ninety men arrested after the Murmansk incident had their sentences reduced as follows: the thirteen sentences of death were commuted to five years, but twelve men were released after only one year, and the other after two years. Twenty men, originally given five years, were released after six months. Fifty-one men sentenced to two years were also released within six months.

Following the announcement, on 22 December 1919, of nineteen of these acts of 'clemency' the First Lord of the Admiralty told the House of Commons that 'bad leadership' was a factor behind the mutiny. He even hinted at the possibility of disciplinary measures being taken against several officers. Smith-Hill was subsequently informed that he had 'incurred the severe displeasure' of the Lords of the Admiralty, but no further action was taken against him, and he eventually left the service as a brigadier. He maintained for the rest of his life that a significant cause of the incident was that most of the officers had only had sea service during the war, and they had received no training for this kind of land warfare.

The disgrace of this mutiny was keenly felt in the corps for many years afterwards. General Sir H.E. Blumberg's 1927 book *Britain's Sea Soldiers*, the most comprehensive account ever published of the involvement of the Royal Marines in the First World War, which goes into almost forensic levels of detail, makes no mention of it. No 6th Battalion was ever subsequently raised.

Chapter Seven

Flying Marines

Although the Royal Marines as a body did not operate aircraft during the First World War, a number of officers from the corps played a significant part in the air campaign between 1914 and 1918. For the most part these officers were seconded to the Royal Naval Air Service. Indeed, the corps has been linked with naval aviation since its earliest days. Naval flying began in 1911, when three Royal Navy officers and a lieutenant of the Royal Marine Light Infantry were permitted by their Lordships of the Admiralty to draw full pay, while being taught to fly at the Royal Aero Club ground at Eastchurch, on three Short biplanes lent by Mr Frank McClean, a member of the club. Dr G.B. Cockburn, another member of the club, gave his services freely as an instructor for some six months, while teaching these officers to fly. When the Royal Flying Corps (RFC) was formed in 1912, these officers, and some three or four others from the navy who had learned to fly at their own expense, were located at Eastchurch as what was at first known as the Naval Wing, RFC. An air department was then formed at the Admiralty, under Captain Murray F. Sueter, RN, who had already been concerned with airship work. From this nucleus, the Naval Wing expanded and it would become in time the Royal Naval Air Service. Coast defence and experimental stations were formed before the war at Calshot, Isle of Grain (Kent), Felixstowe, Yarmouth, and Dundee. Much development and experimentation with seaplanes was carried out here.

The Royal Marine lieutenant who was numbered among the first four pilots to be trained for the Royal Naval Air Service was – later – Air Commodore E.L. Gerrard CMG DSO. On 19 June 1912 the Central Flying School was formed at Upavon, and one of the first instructors was Gerrard. He arrived in August 1912 in his own Nieuport monoplane, which had been granted to him by the Admiralty. The first course included three other Royal Marine officers, lieutenants G.V. Wildman-Lushington and Ivon T. Courtney, and Captain Charles E. Risk. The first of these three was based at Eastney Barracks and was selected as one of the first four naval pilots to be trained in 1911, but owing to other commitments could not take up his place, and so it was during 1912 that he was to be trained as a pilot in the newly created Naval Wing of the Royal Flying Corps. He was promoted to acting captain, flight commander RFC, and based at the RFC airfield in Eastchurch in Kent. Tragically, while piloting a Henry Farman Biplane on 2 December 1913 he was killed while attempting to land at Eastchurch airfield. The aircraft fell into a side slip and hit the ground from 50 feet, being completely destroyed. Risk suffered a similar mishap in 1913 when his carburettor froze at 800 feet and the machine crashed, though he and his observer survived. He later reached the rank of wing commander in seaplanes.

Prior to the war in 1913, Gerrard set up a new British passenger altitude record by carrying two passengers to a height of 8,400 feet in an R.E.7 tractor biplane, powered by a 14-cylinder Gnome rotary engine. During the First World War he commanded the squadron that made the first attack on Germany from the sky on 22 September 1914, when the RNAS launched an air attack from Antwerp on the Zeppelin sheds at Dusseldorf and Cologne. He was flying in BE2a, number '50' (undoubtedly the most famous bomber of 1914, No. 50 was nominally the personal aircraft of Commander C.R. Samson). No. 50 was followed by No. 149, a Sopwith Churchill, No. 169, a Sopwith Tabloid and No. 906, an impressed Sopwith Tractor Biplane. At this early stage of the air war, none of these aircraft bore any marking other than their black serial number on a white patch. In 1915, Gerrard destroyed the Zeppelin L.12. He was later awarded the DSO: 'In recognition of his services in command of a Wing of the RNAS in the Eastern Mediterranean. The present efficiency of this Wing is due very largely to Wing Commander Gerrard, whose personal example and the manner in which he has encouraged the younger officers under his command are all that can be desired.'[1]

He went on to serve with the RAF when it was formed in April 1918. He had joined the Royal Marine Light Infantry in September 1900, and served in the corps until 1919, when he transferred permanently to the RAF.

From the outbreak of war on 4 August 1914, Captain Cecil Francis Kilner RMLI was flying seaplanes on patrol in the North Sea from the RN Air Stations at Clacton and Westgate, and with the detached RNAS Unit at Ostend, but this unit withdrew when the Belgian Garrison retired to Dunkirk. His DSO citation records that:

> On the 25th December 1914, an air reconnaissance of the Heligoland Bight, including Cuxhaven, Heligoland and Wilhemshaven was made by seven naval seaplanes, and the opportunity was taken at the same time of attacking with bombs, points of military importance. The reconnaissance involved combined operations with light cruisers and destroyers, and submarines watching inshore and ready to render aid if necessary.
>
> The vessels detailed having arrived at the rendezvous before daylight, as soon the light was sufficient, the seaplanes were hoisted out (from HMS *Engadine*) and dispatched. At the beginning of the flight the weather was clear, but on nearing land the seaplanes met with thick weather and were compelled to fly low, thus becoming exposed to a heavy fire at a short range. Several machines were hit, but all remained in the air for three hours and succeeded in obtaining valuable information regarding dispositions of the enemy's ships and defences. Bombs were dropped on military points.
>
> Capt. Kilner's and two other machines regained their ship. Three others, short of fuel, were compelled to descend and their pilots were saved by Submarine 'E1' although subjected to fire from an airship. The pilot of the remaining sea plane, having lost his bearings, was compelled to descend after 3 ½ hours flight, owing to engine trouble and was rescued by a Dutch trawler and returned safely to England.[2]

Captain Ivon T. Courtney, RMLI flew in the army manoeuvres of 1913. He arrived in Belgium in late August 1914, with other aircrew from Eastchurch, to form the nucleus of a naval wing guarding the Channel ports and to attack Zeppelin bases, which made its first bombing flight on 14 September. Later he commanded a squadron in the combined landplane and seaplane operations in the Bruges – Ostend – Zeebrugge district, between 11 and 16 February 1915 against enemy submarine bases. He also took part in the raid on the German submarines under construction at Hoboken near Antwerp on 24 March 1915, dropping four bombs from 1,000 feet on the boats and works. He was remembered as a dashing and good-looking officer, who wore an unofficial blue uniform of his own design, which his contemporaries copied and which became the model for the later Marine officers' 'B serge' uniform. He died aged 93 in 1978.

Captain Ivon T. Courtney, Royal Marine Light Infantry (*Author's Collection*)

One of the first pilots to see action was Lieutenant C.H. Collet RMA who was serving in the Eastchurch Wing under Commander Samson, operating on the exposed left flank of the Allied armies near Dunkirk. On 22 September 1914 he took part in the raid of four aircraft against the Zeppelin sheds at Düsseldorf and Cologne. Because of thick mist only Collet reached his target, dropping two 20lb bombs from 400 feet on to the Zeppelin sheds at Düsseldorf. This was the first successful bombing raid ever carried out, and for his exploit Collet was awarded the DSO. The citation read: 'On 22 September 1914, flying a Sopwith Tractor Biplane made a successful attack on the German Zeppelin Airship shed at Dusseldorf. Lieut. Collet's feat is notable – gliding down from 6,000 feet, the last 1,500 in mist, he finally came in sight of the Airship shed at a height of 400 feet, only a quarter of a mile away from it.'[3]

He was sent to Tenedos in March 1915 as part of No. 3 Aeroplane Squadron RNAS, to support the Dardanelles campaign. The main aviation duties were bombardment spotting for the Royal Navy. Unfortunately Lieutenant Collett was later killed, when he had an engine failure on take off and his plane crashed and burnt out. He was buried in a cemetery on the island of Imbros. He was known as the marine with the photographic memory, so accurate that he could play chess blindfolded.

Also present was Kilner, who on 2 February 1915 was appointed to the *Ark Royal* (Seaplane Carrier) for operations in the Eastern

HMS *Ark Royal*, seaplane carrier in the Dardanelles. (*Library of Congress*)

Mediterranean. He was the senior flying officer of the ship and was present at the bombardment of the Dardanelles Forts from 17 February 1915 to 12 March 1915, the attempt to force the Narrows on 18 March 1915, the air raid on Smyrna, and the landings at Anzac and Suvla in April and July 1915.

William Basil Loxdale Jones obtained a commission in the Royal Marine Artillery in 1915. He saw service first in France, and was wounded. He was described as, 'of very poor physique and almost deformed. He would never have passed for military service. He was transported to the Western front in his own car at his own expense.' In May 1915 as with other marines who wished to fly he became an observer in the Royal Naval Air Service, and in August was posted to Gallipoli. Here he was Mentioned in Despatches. In March 1917 he saw service in Italy and was again Mentioned in Despatches. On 7 January 1918 his aircraft came down in the sea whilst on a photographic patrol near Saseno Island. The aircraft's engine had failed and the machine crashed in the Adriatic. His body was not recovered and he is commemorated on the Chatham Naval Memorial.

Commander of all RNAS operations in the eastern Mediterranean in 1915 was Colonel F.H. Sykes, who had an unusual career path. Sykes was a cavalry officer in the King's Hussars before becoming interested in flying, and transferring to the RFC. In 1915 he was sent by the Admiralty to oversee the somewhat freelance operations of the RNAS in the Aegean. In order to do this he was given a commission in the Royal Marines as colonel (temporary wing captain RNAS). On conclusion of the Dardanelles campaign in March 1916 he resigned his commission in the Marines, but he later became Chief of the Air Staff on formation of the RAF, before Sir Hugh Trenchard finally assumed this office.

Royal Marine officers were also active in the air in other theatres of war. *Flight International Magazine* of 15 December 1915 made reference to the difficulties experienced in East Africa, operating against a German battleship, when it quoted from the Dispatch of Vice Admiral H. King-Hall commanding the Cape of Good Hope station:

> Most serious risks have been run by the officers and men who have flown in this climate, where the effect of the atmosphere and the extreme heat of the sun are quite unknown to those whose flying experience is limited to moderate climates. 'Bumps' of 250 feet have been experienced several times, and the temperature varies from extreme cold when flying at a height to a great heat, with burning, tropical sun, when on land. In the operations against the 'Königsberg' on July 6th both personnel and materiel of the Royal Naval Air Service were worked to the extreme limit of endurance. The total distance covered by the two available aeroplanes on that date was no less than 950 miles, and the time in the air, working watch and watch, was 13 hours. Acting Lieutenant Alan G. Bishop, Royal Marine Light Infantry, of H.M.S. 'Hyacinth.' This officer volunteered to observe during the second attack on the 'Königsberg,' though he had had no previous experience of flying.[4]

Additionally, Air Mechanic Ebenezer Henry Alexander Boggis (service number Chatham 14849), had gone up on 25 April 1915 with Flight Commander Cull, and photographed the *Königsberg* at a height of 700 feet. They were heavily fired on, and the engine of the machine was badly damaged. Boggis had enlisted in the Royal Marine Light Infantry in 1904 but according to his service record had been seconded to the RFC in 1913. In 1914 his rank is recorded as air mechanic. By 1916 he was a petty officer Mechanic and by 1918 was a chief petty officer when eventually he transferred to the RAF.

In command of the air operations against the *Königsberg* was Wing Captain (later Air Commodore) Robert Gordon DSO, who was a captain of Royal Marine Light Infantry when he learned to fly at Brooklands on a Bristol box-kite early in 1911. Thereafter he flew a Breguet at Eastchurch, and later Dundee Air Station. Later in the war he did exceptionally fine work in command of RNAS units in Mesopotamia, attempting to fly food and supplies to the beleaguered garrison at Kut.

Major Henry Fawcett began the war engaged in coastal patrols in the North Sea, in seaplane squadrons and later served in the Dardanelles. In No. 3 Wing he operated from Imbros with the seaplanes from HMS *Ark Royal* during the withdrawal from Gallipoli, and carried out reconnaissance flights in the Salonika area. Born on 28 February 1884, in San Antonio, Texas he received his first commission in the Royal Marine Light Infantry on 1 January 1902. Promoted lieutenant on 1 January 1903, and captain on 1 January 1913, he became a field officer on 1 January 1918. He became interested in flying in 1912, and flew for his pilot's certificate on 3 June

The German cruiser SMS *Königsberg*, wrecked in the Rufiji river delta, East Africa, 1915. (*Public Domain*)

1913, at the Central Flying School, Upavon. Immediately afterwards he was posted to the RNAS. On 3 December 1913, while flying with Captain Wildman-Lushington, RMA, he was seriously injured in the crash in which the latter as pilot was killed. A rear seat passenger, Captain Henry Fawcett, Royal Marine Light Infantry, survived the crash suffering only light injuries, emerging from the wreckage in a dazed condition. This type of aircraft was of extremely flimsy design as were many of the early 'Flying Machines' of that era. The fliers and pilots were extremely brave men to leave the ground in what became known as 'Stringbag Kites' and Wildman-Lushington had a reputation as a daring and capable airman at the time.

Fawcett spent a period of time in fighter duties, operating from Dunkirk on the Western Front, under the command of the RFC. He was the first commander of 9 Squadron RNAS, upon its formation, but most of No. 9 Squadron's officers were draw from training establishments in England – unfortunately seniority gained from home service at Cranwell, Eastchurch and Chingford did not make for good combat pilots. A lack of aggression, combined with a dreadful reputation for machine serviceability, came to a head whilst the squadron was on secondment to the RFC – a patrol was abandoned after every single pilot dropped out with mechanical problems.

Fawcett was the sacrificial lamb and was 'returned to unit' to appease the RFC. He also suffered the humiliation of being reduced in rank, though he was soon promoted once more to major. There is little doubt that RNAS policy resulted in No. 9 Squadron suffering in order to keep No. 3 Squadron fully manned, however, Fawcett does not seem to have grasped the management aspects of keeping the squadron in the air. He also failed to recognise which of his pilots were good, and which were not, allowing incompetent and timid flight commanders to continue in position for far too long. A friend remembered:

> My first meeting with him was in 1915, when he commanded the advance party of No. 2 Wing, R.N.A.S, at Imbros. His health was unsatisfactory and his moods changed with great rapidity. From moody depression he would change in an instant to a happy period of great personal charm. His worldly knowledge was wide and his professional pride keen. The powers that be were never deified in

his mind, and his flying career suffered accordingly. He was a true-hearted and gallant friend who gave the best in his life to the service he loved. After the Dardanelles expedition he served in France as a Squadron Commander employed with the Army, and at home in command of the air station at Redcar. On August 22nd, 1917, he returned to his regiment, with which he was serving at the time of his death.[5]

Major Henry Fawcett was accidentally shot and killed at Murmansk during the operations in north Russia, whilst commanding the Royal Marines contingent there. He was head of naval intelligence, and had agents active in Finland and Petrograd. There were many people who mourned the death of Henry Fawcett. During his many years of service he made innumerable friends in both the army and the navy.

Lieutenant J.H. d'Albiac served in the famous naval Eight Squadron RNAS as an observer at Dunkirk and gained a DSO as an observer with them in June 1916. Like nearly all the other Marine officers described here he transferred to the RAF on its formation. J.H. d'Albiac was however by far the most distinguished flying Royal Marine officer of this era. He went on to command all British forces in Greece in 1941 during Wavell's campaign in the Second World War. He retired in 1947 as Air Marshal Sir John d'Albiac to become commandant of London's Heathrow Airport.

Air Commodore C.E.H. Rathborne joined the Royal Flying Corps (Naval Wing) in April 1913, from the Royal Marine Light Infantry. During the First World War he served in France with the Royal Naval Air Service and the Royal Air Force and was awarded the DSO in recognition of his gallantry and devotion to duty, whilst taking part in a long-distance air raid in which his engine was put out of action and he was taken prisoner. The awarded was gazetted on 17 January 1919 (rank shown as captain RMLI; wing commander RNAS), the citation reading:

> In recognition of his gallantry and devotion to duty during the course of a long distance air raid in which he acted as a pilot of a fighting machine which formed part of the escort. Wing Commander Rathborne was brought down whilst protecting the bombing machines, his engine having been put out of action. It was owing

to the gallantry and self-sacrifice of this officer and those of other fighting machines that all the bombing machines returned safely from the raid.[6]

He subsequently escaped from captivity and was awarded a Bar to his DSO. He was appointed to a permanent commission in the Royal Air Force in 1919, and later commanded Royal Air Force units at home and in Iraq. He became Chief Staff Officer, Inland Area, in October 1930 and was promoted Air Commodore in January 1931.

From the outbreak of the First World War he was in charge of seaplanes operating from Dunkirk until joining the Independent Air Force in France. In 1918, Rathbone provided a statement to a British commission of enquiry into conditions in German PoW camps. It read:

> I was captured on 14 April 1917, and was sent to Colmar for 18 days, and then to Karlsruhe where I remained till September. I was then sent to Holzminden. I was moved to Schweidnitz on 8th December, and escaped from there in March 1918. I was recaptured and sent back to Holzminden, from where I finally escaped on 23rd June 1918.
>
> With regard to Schweidnitz, the great drawback to this camp is the complete lack of space for exercise. When I was there we occupied a single building, which had been a workhouse. We had the run of a good sized orchard, but it was planted all over with fruit trees, so that games were impossible. There were about 300 officers in the camp, and we were badly cramped indoors too.
>
> There were as many as 50 all sleeping in one room, and as there was no reading-room of any sort, one had no quiet or privacy for study. The dining hall had to serve for every purpose. Otherwise Schweidnitz was a well-managed camp, though the Commandant (whose name was something like Kopenik) was not obliging nor particularly polite. For instance, when we tried to hire a football field he forbade it, and told us plainly he was not there to do us favours.[7]

On 1 February 1932 Air Commodore Charles Edward Henry Rathborne, then senior air staff officer, Inland Area, became air officer commanding, Royal Air Force, Mediterranean.

A most original character who was worthy of note was the late Colonel T.H. Orde-Lees OBE AFC. On the outbreak of the First World War he was given leave of absence to join Sir Ernest Shackleton's expedition to the Antarctic. On his return he was seconded to the RFC, where he applied his personal courage and great powers of invention in demonstrating new methods of parachute jumping. At the time it was not compulsory for pilots to carry parachutes. Despite official inertia and scepticism he was determined that pilots should have them. To this end he demonstrated the virtues of an improved parachute by making spectacular jumps himself from Tower Bridge and elsewhere. After a long campaign of persuasion, the authorities were finally convinced and Orde-Lees was awarded the AFC in 1919. Orde-Lees and A.C. Morford were the only Royal Marine officers seconded to the RFC during the 1914–1918 war to carry out purely military as opposed to naval flying. Morford, whose recklessness became legendary, returned to the Marines in 1918.

Wing Commander C.E.H. Rathborne, Royal Marine Light Infantry
(*Author's Collection*)

Godfrey Edward Wildman-Lushington was the brother of Captain Gilbert Vernon Wildman-Lushington of the Royal Marine Artillery. The death of Wildman-Lushington before the war did not deter his brother for taking up aviation, and Godfrey Edward, also of the RMA, was promoted to lieutenant in 1915. He gained his aviator's certificate in 1916. In August of that year he was appointed probationary flight sub-lieutenant for attachment to the RNAS, and was appointed to HMS *President*. After service in HMS *Swiftsure* 1915/1916 in which he saw action in the Dardanelles and Suvla Bay, he transferred to the RNAS in January 1917, where he had continuous flying duty until 1919. He qualified as a seaplane and flying boat pilot and flew operationally in anti submarine patrols from Calshot, Plymouth, Cattewater and Newlyn. He continued with this until the end of the war and received a Mention in Despatches. On one occasion, on 20 December 1917 he was flying a

Short seaplane on patrol about 45 miles south-west of Plymouth with B.E. Harrison (later wing commander AFC) as observer. Suddenly an explosion occurred in the engine, which burst into flames. With great skill he sideslipped to avoid the flames and alighted on the sea where they succeeded in putting out the fire. For over an hour there was no sign of help when fortunately, a Greek cargo ship, SS *Kanasis*, appeared. They managed to signal it with their Aldis lamp and after some suspicion they were picked up and taken to Falmouth. Wildman-Lushington had a distinguished post-war career and was appointed head of combined operations, working alongside Lord Mountbatten. He retired with the rank of lieutenant general.

Lionel Edwin Innes-Baillie served in the RMA from 12 December 1914 to 2 February 1915 at Eastney, and was appointed to the RNAS from 3 February 1915 to 31 March 1918. Navy lists show that in May 1915 he was serving in No. 1 Squadron RNAS as an observer. In April 1917 he was at Dunkirk, and in April 1918 he was at Eastchurch. The fact that he was awarded the Legion of Honour at the end of the war by the French indicates that he performed the job of observer with some credit, since very few of these received decorations. He transferred to the RAF on 1 April 1918, but his further career cannot be traced. He is absent from the air force list for January 1923.

It is believed that the Royal Marines officers who served as air crew in the First World War between them gained nine awards of the DSO, three CMG, one CBE, and two AFC. On the formation of the Royal Air Force in 1918, ten of them transferred to the RAF, namely Bishop, Courtney, d'Albiac, Gerrard, Gordon, Innes-Baillie, Kilner, Rathborne, Risk and Ward. Of these, one became wing commander, two became group captains, four air commodores and one an air marshal. In addition, F.H. Sykes, who had returned to the army, became the first chief of the air staff.

Notes

Introduction
1. *Oxfordshire Weekly News,* 25 August 1915
2. Jon E. Lewis *Mammoth Book of War Diaries and Letters,* London, 1998, p.250
3. G. Bird, manuscript letter, February 1915. Liddle Collection, University of Leeds
4. *Gloucester Journal,* 19 June 1915

Chapter One
1. Anon, *500 of the Best Cockney War Stories,* London, nd, p.166
2. George Aston, *Secret Service,* London 1930, p.68
3. Lewis, *Mammoth Book of War Diaries and Letters,* p.250
4. John Cusack, *Scarlet Fever A Lifetime With Horses*, London, 1972, p.46
5. Edward Page, *Escaping from Germany*, London, 1919, p.6
6. Op cit
7. Page, *Escaping from Germany,* p.11
8. Page, *Escaping from Germany,* p.12
9. *Staffordshire Sentinel*, 16 October 1914
10. Walter Newman Flower, *The Boy Who Did Grow Up,* London, 1919, p.180
11. The National Archives WO 161/99/71
12. The National Archives WO 161/98/206
13. The National Archives WO 161/98/636
14. *Sunderland Daily Echo and Shipping Gazette,* 24 October 1914
15. *Belfast Telegraph,* 10 November 1914
16. *Walsall Advertiser,* 24 October 1914
17. *Glossop-dale Chronicle and North Derbyshire Reporter,* 8 January 1915
18. *Leicester Chronicle,* 17 October 1914
19. *West Middlesex Gazette,* 16 October 1914
20. *Burton Chronicle,* 15 October 1914
21. *Evening News* (London), 26 October 1914

Chapter Two
1. *Belper News,* 9 April 1915
2. Private Harry Baker, Chatham Battalion, Royal Marine Brigade – Imperial War Museum interview
3. *Bucks Herald,* 29 May 1915
4. *Stapleford & Sandiacre News,* 25 March 1919
5. *Hampshire Telegraph,* 1 October 1915

6. *Chester Chronicle,* 11 September 1915
7. John Lewis-Stempel, *The Autobiography of the British Soldier: From Agincourt to Basra, in His Own Words,* London, 2007, p.259
8. *Ripley and Heanor News and Ilkeston Division Free Press,* 16 July 1915
9. Compton Mackenzie, *Gallipoli Memories* New York, 1930, p.20
10. Peter Liddle, *Men of Gallipoli,* London, 1976, p.179
11. Liddle, *op cit*
12. Mackenzie, p.120
13. *Derbyshire Courier,* 13 July 1915
14. *Mansfield Reporter,* 6 August 1915
15. *Chester Chronicle,* 11 September 1915
16. *Staffordshire Sentinel,* 2 August 1915
17. *Birkenhead News,* 14 August 1915
18. http://www.hellfirecorner.co.uk/clegg.htm
19. Nigel McCrery, *Into Touch: Rugby Internationals killed in the Great War,* Barnsley, 2022 p.159
20. *Penistone, Stocksbridge and Hoyland Express,* 25 December 1915
21. http://www.hellfirecorner.co.uk/clegg.htm
22. *Chester Chronicle,* 12 May 1917

Chapter Three

1. *Belfast Weekly Telegraph,* 30 January 1915
2. *Burnley News,* 24 October 1914
3. *Bromsgrove & Droitwich Messenger,* 17 October 1914
4. *Bromsgrove & Droitwich Messenger,* 12 June 1915
5. *Liverpool Echo,* 1 October 1914
6. *The Times,* 22 October 1996
7. Liddle, *Men of Gallipoli,* p.41
8. *Royal Naval Division* magazine (private publication L. Sellers), issue number 19, pp. 1870–1874
9. *Hampshire Telegraph,* 1 October 1915
10. Oppenheim journal, Royal Marines Museum archives 11/13/034
11. Op cit
12. Op cit
13. Op cit
14. Op cit
15. *Broad Arrow,* 2 July 1915
16. Stephen Snelling, *VCs of the First World War: The Naval VCs,* Cheltenham, 2013, p.108
17. Jon Sutherland, *The Battle of Jutland,* Barnsley, 2014, p.115
18. Archibald Hurd *The Heroic Record of the British Navy,* New York, 1919, p.77
19. *Thanet Advertiser,* 4 August 1917
20. Samuel Bassett, *Royal Marine; The Autobiography of Colonel Sam Bassett,* New York, 1965, p.52

21. *The Cornishman,* 12 June 1918
22. *London Gazette,* 7 January 1919
23. Anon, *500 of the Best Cockney War Stories,* p.207

Chapter Four
1. *West Briton and Cornwall Advertiser,* 2 December 1915
2. Op cit
3. *Ballymena Weekly Telegraph,* 11 September 1915
4. Anon, *500 of the Best Cockney War Stories,* p.35
5. Jeremy Archer *Home For Christmas,* London, 2007, p.56
6. *First Aid on Shore with the Royal Naval Division* in *Journal of the Royal Naval Medical Service. Vol. 7, 1921*
7. Geoffrey Sparrow, *On Four Fronts with the Royal Naval Division,* London, 1918, p.175
8. Sparrow, *On Four Fronts,* p.177
9. The National Archives WO 95/3110/2
10. The National Archives WO 161/99/207
11. The National Archives WO 161/100/113
12. *Chester Chronicle,* 12 May 1917
13. Op cit
14. John Brough, *A Marine in the Great War,* Brighton, 2012, p.93
15. *Hampshire Telegraph,* 16 November 1917
16. *Blackwoods Magazine,* June 1919, Vol. 205, Issue 1244, p.791 *Courts Martial in France*
17. The National Archives WO 161/100/143
18. The National Archives WO 161/100/194
19. The National Archives WO 161/100/184
20. Anon, *500 of the Best Cockney War Stories,* p.76
21. *Birkenhead News,* 19 October 1918
22. Max Arthur, *The True Glory: The Royal Navy, 1914–1939,* London, 1996, p.58
23. Julian Thompson, *The Royal Marines: From Sea Soldiers to Special Force,* London, 2000, p.201

Chapter Five
1. Julian Thompson, *The Imperial War Museum Book of The War At Sea 1914–1918,* London, 2005, p.406
2. Paul Kendall, *Voices from the Past: The Zeebrugge Raid 1918,* Barnsley, 2016, p.69
3. Susan Holloway, *From Trench and Turret: Royal Marines' Letters and Diaries 1914–18,* London, 2006, p.166
4. *Derby Daily Telegraph,* 24 April 1918
5. Op cit
6. Holloway, *From Trench and Turret,* p.170
7. John Wells, *The Royal Navy, An Illustrated Social History 1870–1982* Stroud, 1994, p.122

8. Thompson, *Imperial War Museum Book of the War at Sea*, p.418
9. M.J. Crook, *The Evolution of the Victoria Cross* Tunbridge Wells, 1975, p.114
10. James Lewis Moulton, *The Royal Marines* London, 1972, p.63
11. Moulton, *The Royal Marines* p.63

Chapter Six
1. Anon, *500 of the Best Cockney War Stories,* p.109
2. *London Gazette,* 20 October 1920
3. *Dundee Evening Telegraph,* 19 August 1920
4. Max Arthur, *Lost Voices of the Royal Navy,* London, 2005, p.159
5. Mark Bentinck, *Mutiny in Murmansk, The Hidden Shame, Royal Marines Historical Society, Special Publication No. 21,* Portsmouth, nd
6. *Daily Herald,* 28 November 1919
7. Op cit

Chapter Seven
1. *London Gazette,* 22 Jun 1916
2. *London Gazette,* 19 February 1915
3. *London Gazette,* 23 October 1914
4. *Flight International,* 15 December 1915
5. *The Aeroplane,* 22 January 1919
6. *London Gazette,* 17 January 1919
7. The National Archives, WO 161/96/118

Bibliography

Anon, *500 of the Best Cockney War Stories,* London, nd
Archer, Jeremy, *Home For Christmas,* London, 2007
Arthur, Max, *Lost Voices of the Royal Navy,* London, 2005
Arthur, Max, *Forgotten Voices of the Great War,* London, 2002
Arthur, Max, *The True Glory: The Royal Navy, 1914–1939,* London, 1996
Aston, George *Secret Service,* London, 1930
Bassett, Samuel John Woodruff, *Royal Marine; The Autobiography of Colonel Sam Bassett,* New York, 1965
Bittner, Donald F., *'Good Men Wasted … Dreadful!!!' Two Royal Marine Officer's Commentaries on Gallipoli, March-August 1915,* in *Journal of the Society for Army Historical Research,* winter 2005, Vol. 83, No. 336, pp.309–326
Blumberg, H.E., *Britain's Sea Soldiers,* Devonport, 1927
Brough, John, *A Marine in the Great War,* Brighton, 2012
Bruckshaw, Horace, *The Diaries of Private Horace Bruckshaw,* edited and introduced by Martin Middlebrook, London, 1979
Copplestone, Bennet, *British Royal Marines, A Corps of Improvisors, Ready and Efficient Alike on Sea and Land in Sea Power.* Vols. 7–8, 1919–1920. Washington, DC, Sea Power Pub. Co
Crook, M.J., *The Evolution of the Victoria Cross,* Tunbridge Wells, 1975
Flower, Walter Newman, *The Boy Who Did Grow Up,* London, 1919
Holloway, Susan, *From Trench and Turret: Royal Marines' Letters and Diaries 1914–18,* London, 2006
Hurd, Archibald, *The Heroic Record of the British Navy,* New York, 1919
Kendall, Paul, *Voices from the Past: The Zeebrugge Raid 1918,* Barnsley, 2016,
Liddle, Peter, *Men of Gallipoli,* London, 1976
McCrery, Nigel, *Into Touch: Rugby Internationals killed in the Great War,* Barnsley, 2022
Mackenzie, Compton, *Gallipoli Memories,* New York, 1930
Marsh, Alan, *Flying Marines,* Portsmouth, 1980
Moulton, James Lewis, *The Royal Marines,* London, 1972
Page, Edward, *Escaping from Germany,* London, 1919
Richardson, Matthew, *1914: Voices from the Battlefields,* Barnsley, 2013
Reece, Michael, *Flying Royal Marines,* Southsea, 2012
Smith, Peter Charles, *Per Mare Per Terram,* St Ives, Hunts, 1974
Snelling, Stephen, *VCs of the First World War: The Naval VCs,* Cheltenham, 2013
Sparrow, Geoffrey & Macbean Ross, J. N., *On Four Fronts with the Royal Naval Division,* London, 1918

Spector, Ronald H., *At War, At Sea: Sailors and Naval Combat in the Twentieth Century,* New York, 2001

Sutherland, Jon & Canwell, Diane, *The Battle of Jutland,* Barnsley, 2014

Thompson, Julian, *The Imperial War Museum Book of The War At Sea 1914–1918,* London, 2005

Thompson, Julian, *The Royal Marines: From Sea Soldiers to Special Force,* London, 2000

Wells, John, *The Royal Navy, An Illustrated Social History 1870–1982,* Stroud, 1994

Wright, Damien, *Churchill's Secret War with Lenin,* Solihull, 2017

Index

1st Battalion Royal Marines, 91, 92, 95-97, 104, 107, 110–11, 128
2nd Battalion Royal Marines, 91–9, 104–107
3rd battalion Royal Marines, 91, 108
4th battalion Royal Marines, 115–16, 123
6th battalion Royal Marines, 126, 130

Andrews, C.B., 35–6
Anti-Aircraft Brigade, 90
Antwerp, 1, 3, 6, 10, 14, 16, 20–1, 34, 100, 111
Appleton, Herbert, **6**
Archangel, 124–5
Armoured cars, 3–5
Aston, Maj. Gen. Sir George, 2
Asquith, Lieutenant, 24–5

Baker, Harry, 28–9
Bamford, Edward, 121
Bandsmen, 21–2, 25, 73, **87**
Barbados, **78**, 79
Barber, George Frederick, **52**
Barnby, Major A.C., 128, 130
Barnes, Jack Clixby, 36
Bassett, Sam, 74, 80
Bath, Captain, 126
Black, Cecil J.T., 35
Bedall-Sivright, David Revell, 49–50
Belgium, 3, 6, 8, 21, 25, 100
Bell (Private), 18–19
Bell, H., 17–18
Billings, Stanley, **25**
Bilson, Thomas, 1, 2
Bird, George, *x*, **44**
Bird, J., 19–20
Bishop, Lieutenant Alan G., 138
Blades, Herbert, 48
Blumberg, General Sir H.E., 132
Boggis, Ebenezer Henry Alexander, 138–9

Brooks, Benjamin, 20
Brough, John, 99, **100**
Bruckshaw, Horace, 34–5
Budd, John, 62
Burton, T.H., 111
Buses, 4, **5, 16**

Calverley, George, 119–21
Cameroons, 57–60
Chandler, J., 17
Chappell, Heber, 18
Chatham, *vii*, 7, 74, 82, 115, 128, 131, 137
Chatham battalion, 1, **12, 18**, 29, **31**, 33, 36, 43–5, **50**
Chesterfield, 27
Churchill, Winston Spencer, 6–8, 25–6, 74, 89
Clark, Herbert A., **89**
Clegg, John, 49–51
Collett, Lieutenant C.H., 136
Cooper, Wilfred Wheatley, 26
Coronel, Battle of, 56
Court Martial, 129–31
Courtney, Lieutenant Ivon T., 134–5, **136**

D'Albiac, Lieutenant J.H., 141, 144
Daily Herald, 131
Dardanelles, *ix, x,* 15, 26, 130, 136–7, 143
Day, Harry, 82, 84–5
Deal, 86–8, 114, 122–3
Deans, Thomas, 91
Dempsey, Michael, 105
Distinguished Conduct Medal, 92, 127
Doberitz, 17–18
Dunkirk, 3, 7–8, 25, 102–103, 135–6, 140–2, 144

Elliot, Bertram, 115
Evans, B., 60–1
Evans, George Elliott, 48

Fawcett, Major Henry, 139–41
Feeney, James, 119
Fielder, B.J., *x*, 3
Finch, George, 61–2, 122
Finch, Norman Augustus, 121–2

Gale, Reginald M., 38–9
Gallipoli *see* Dardanelles
Gasson, Bryan, 75
Gavrelle, Battle of, 96
Gerrard, Air Commodore E.L., 133
Goodman, F. Edgar, 72
Gordon, Wing Captain Robert, 139
Gouldsmith, Philip, 18
Grant, D.L., 104

Hague, Harry, **101**
Hall, George, 14
Hardstaff, George, 92
Harries, Lieutenant, 124
Harrison, Sydney, 43
Harvey, Francis John William, **73**, 74
Herford, Bernard Henry, **31**
Herrod, John, 44
Hobbs, Ernest, 107–108
Hodgeson, Philip, 115
Horne, Harold, 110
Hulme, Thomas Ernest, 103
Hutchinson, George Arthur, 44, **47**

Innes-Baillie, Lionel Edwin, 144
Internment, 19–21

Jaggers, George, 27
Jameson, Tom, 43, 126
Jones, William Basil Loxdale, 137
Jutland, Battle of, 73, 122

Kenney, George James, 15
Keyes, Roger Vice Admiral, 112, 115, 119, 122
Kilner, Captain Cecil Francis, 135–6
King, Arthur G., 22
King's Badge, 123
King's Squad, 123
Kitkat, Lieutenant-Colonel A. de W., 127, 129

Laing, Major R.W., 129
Litchfield, Thomas William, **50**
Lockwood, Walter, 16
Lowe, George, 85

MacBean-Ross, J.N., 93–4
McClure, T.Y., 106
Mackenzie, Compton, 37–42
Maher, J.J., **31**
Marder, Arthur, 123
Marriott, Charles, **122**
Marsden, Roland, **94**
Mayes, Charles, 57
Meatyard, William, 65–7, 94–5
Merchant, Lieutenant, 124
Morale, *x*, 21, 27, 44, 53, 56, 122, 127
Morford, A.C., 143
Morgan, Fred, 53–5
Mulloy, Anthony, 109
Murmansk, 125–6, 132, 141
Mutiny, 130–2

Nelson, Joseph William, **98**
Nettleton, George Edwin Howard, 92
Newling, Second Lieutenant, 97
Nichols, Bertram, 97

Oppenheim, Godfrey, 69–71
Orde-Lees, Colonel T.H., 143
Osmaston, C.A., 90
Ostend, 1, 102, 112, 135

Page, Arthur, 101
Page, Edward, 7–11, **12**
Parker, Walter, 30
Plymouth Battalion, 1, 16, 20, 27, **32**, 34, 36, 46–7, 91
Portsmouth Battalion, 1, **6**, 26, 30, 35, 43, **44**, 50, **52**
Potts, Bertram, 36–7
Powell, F., 68–9
Prince, Albert, 46
Prisoners of war, 16, 97–8, 100, 104–106, 126, 128, 142
Pyle, Thomas, 127–8, **129**

Rathborne, Air Commodore C.E.H., 141–2, **143**, 144

Rawson, A.C., 50
Reed, Stanley C., 63
Ridings, Major A.W., 127
Risk, Captain Charles E., 134
Robinson, Franks Lubbock, 89
Robinson, Ralph, 108
Royal Marine Artillery, vii, 1, 88, **89**, 90–1, 101, **102**, 103, **104, 113,** 121, 125, 143
Royal Marine Light Infantry, vii, 3, 114, 122, 125, 133
Royal Marines Police, 62
Royal Naval Air Service, 3, 133, 140–1
Royal Naval Division, 3, 7, 17, 91, 99–100, 104
Russia, *x*, 124–31, 141

St.John Ambulance Brigade, 12
Samson, Charles Rumney, 3, **4,** 134
Scapa Flow, **83**
Scorey, Bill, 116, 118
Schofield, John William, 55
Shaw, Fred, 7, 8, 33, 44, 52, 98, 99
Ships:
    Aboukir, HMS, 56
    Agamemnon, HMS, 71
    Ark Royal HMS, 136, **137,** 139
    Badger, HMS, 75
    Black Prince, HMS, 76
    Blenheim, HMS, 72
    Breslau, SMS, 53–4
    Britannia, HMS, 82, 85
    Bulwark, HMS, 62
    Cochrane, HMS, 124
    Cornwall, HMS, 75
    Cornwallis, HMS, 28
    Cressy, HMS, 56
    Cumberland, HMS, 57
    Curacoa, HMS, **84**
    Czar SS, 126
    Daffodil, SS, 112, 114–15, 120
    Defence, HMS, 76
    Drake, HMS, 78
    Dwarf, HMS, 58–60
    Emden, SMS, 60
    Engadine, HMS, 135
    Formidable, HMS, 62–3
    Glasgow, HMS, 75
    Glory, HMS, 124
    Goeben, SMS, 53–4
    Good Hope, HMS, 56
    Highflyer, HMS, *x*
    Hogue, HMS, 56
    Hunsgrove, SS, 81, 82
    Hyacinth, HMS, 138
    Indefatigable, HMS, 76
    Inflexible, HMS, 65, 67
    Invincible, HMS, 74–6
    Irresistible, HMS, 63, 65, 67, **68**
    Iris, SS, 112, 114–15, 119
    Isis, HMS, 80
    Ivernia, SS, 39
    Kanasis SS, 144
    Kent, HMS, 56, 126
    Konigsberg, 76, 138, **139**
    Laurentic, HMS, 76–7
    Leipzig, 75
    Letitia HMHS, 29
    Lion, HMS, 73–4
    Lord Nelson, HMS, 65
    Lutzow, 74, 76
    Monmouth, HMS, 56
    Nurnburg, 56
    Ocean, HMS, 65
    Olympic, SS, 78
    Oropesa, HMS, 61
    Prince George, HMS, 55
    Prince of Wales, HMS, 69–70, 72
    Queen Mary, HMS, 76
    Royal George, 49
    Scorpion, HMS, 65
    Soudan, 67
    Suffolk, HMS, 126
    Swiftsure, HMS, 143
    Triumph, HMS, 72
    Vengeance, HMS, 62, 65
    Vindictive, HMS, 112, 114–16, 118, **119–20,** 121
    Warrior, HMS, 53–4, 76
    Wildfire, HMS, 74
    Wolverine, HMS, 65

Short Service recruits, 26, 43
Shubrick, Major C.L., 10
Smith, A.G., 13
Smith-Hill, Roy, 126–32
Somme, Battle of the, 90–2

Sparrow, Geoffrey, 94–5
Staite, Thomas, 9, 11
Sykes, Colonel F.H., 137–8

Thomas, G., 24–5
Thorne, H., 98
Topliss, William Hugh, 24
Trenchard, Sir Hugh, 138
Trotman, Hubert, 108–10
Tully, Alban Charles, 17
Turnbull, Sergeant, 65

U-boats, 78, 80, 81, 112

Victoria Cross, 30, 73–4, 121–2
Vivian, E. Charles, viii

Walter, George William, **56**
Wanstead Battery, **78, 80**

Watts, P.S., 105
Watts, Captain Reginald Hanhart, 130
Went, Frederick A.M., 76–7
Whittaker, Private, 76
Wilding, Anthony Frederick, **8**
Wildman-Lushington, Lieutenant G.V., 133, 140
Wildman-Lushington, Godfrey Edward, 143
Williamson, Bert, x
Willis, Edgar Stanley, 96
Wright, Harry, 57–8, 121

Ypres, Third Battle of, 99–100

Zeebrugge, 112–13, 116, 122–3

Dear Reader,

We hope you have enjoyed this book, but why not share your views on social media? You can also follow our pages to see more about our other products: facebook.com/penandswordbooks or follow us on X @penswordbooks

You can also view our products at www.pen-and-sword.co.uk (UK and ROW) or www.penandswordbooks.com (North America).

To keep up to date with our latest releases and online catalogues, please sign up to our newsletter at: www.pen-and-sword.co.uk/newsletter

If you would like a printed catalogue with our latest books, then please email: enquiries@pen-and-sword.co.uk or telephone: 01226 734555 (UK and ROW) or email: uspen-and-sword@casematepublishers.com or telephone: (610) 853-9131 (North America).

We respect your privacy and we will only use personal information to send you information about our products.

Thank you!